Rethinking the second language listening test

British Council Monographs on Modern Language Testing

Series Editors: Barry O'Sullivan and Vivien Berry, both at The British Council

This series – published in cooperation with the British Council – provides short books in the area of language testing. These titles are written by well known language testing scholars from across the world and members of the British Councils' Assessment Research Group (ARG). The books offer both a theoretical and a practical perspective to language testing and assessment – proposing, where required, models of development, which are reflected in actual test tasks. They are unique in that they are authored by individuals with considerable academic, teaching and assessment experience, thus offering the reader a unique insight into the link between theory and practice in the area. In many cases, the books illustrate their approach with reference to actual test items, from the British Council's Aptis test service.

Published:

Assessing the language of young learners
Angela Hasselgreen and Gwendydd Caudwell

Forthcoming:

Validity: Theoretical development and integrated arguments
Micheline Chalhoub-Deville and Barry O'Sullivan

RETHINKING THE SECOND LANGUAGE LISTENING TEST:

From theory to practice

John Field

SHEFFIELD UK   BRISTOL CT

Published by Equinox Publishing Ltd.

UK: Office 415, The Workstation, 15 Paternoster Row, Sheffield, South Yorkshire,
          S1 2BX
USA: ISD, 70 Enterprise Drive, Bristol, CT 06010

www.equinoxpub.com

First published 2019

British Library Cataloguing-in-Publication Data

A catalogue record for this book is available from the British Library.

ISBN-13 978 1 78179 714 3 (hardback)
        978 1 78179 715 0 (paperback)
        978 1 78179 716 7 (ePDF)

Library of Congress Cataloging-in-Publication Data

Names: Field, John, date.
Title: Rethinking the second language listening test : from theory to
   practice / John Field.
Description: Bristol, CT : Equinox Publishing, [2019] | Series: British
   Council monographs on modern language testing | Includes bibliographical
   references and index.
Identifiers: LCCN 2018001730 (print) | LCCN 2018006123 (ebook) | ISBN
   9781781797167 (ePDF) | ISBN 9781781797143 (hardcover) | ISBN 9781781797150
   (softcover)
Subjects: LCSH: Second language acquisition—Ability testing. |
   Listening—Study and teaching. | Test-taking skills. | Language and
   language—Study and teaching—Evaluation | Language and languages—Ability
   testing.
Classification: LCC P53.47 (ebook) | LCC P53.47 .F55 2018 (print) | DDC
   418.0076—dc23
LC record available at https://lccn.loc.gov/2018001730

Typeset by S.J.I. Services, New Delhi, India

CONTENTS

List of figures

List of tables

ACKNOWLEDGEMENTS

I owe a great debt of gratitude to the British Council for their financial support for the writing of this book, without which it might never have come to fruition. I am especially grateful to Barry O'Sullivan, Head of Assessment Research and Development at the Council, and Vivien Berry, Senior Researcher for English Language Assessment and editor of this series, for their support and advice during its development.

Much of the mapping from theory to concrete applications had its origins in a review of the British Council's own listening test which I undertook some four years ago. I am grateful to the Aptis Test Production team, Kevin Rutherford and John Tucker, for some productive discussions – in particular, for challenging me to put forward detailed arguments in support of recommendations on areas such as speech rate, accents and vocabulary selection, which ran counter to conventional truisms in the testing of L2 listening. These rationales were the origin of some of the sections that follow. One of the issues discussed with the Council team was the practicality of calculating the density and complexity of idea units in a listening text as an alternative to simple specifications of length. This gave rise to the small-scale project reported in Chapter 11, for which John Tucker undertook much of the data analysis.

I would also like to express my appreciation to CRELLA (the Centre for Research in English Language Learning and Assessment) for providing such a supportive and well-informed environment within which to work. I am constantly indebted to colleagues there for insights into the theory and practice of language testing; and I am especially grateful to Cyril Weir for reading through the final draft of this book. Particular thanks are due too to Luke Harding of the University of Lancaster who reviewed a first draft and provided some useful feedback.

I can never finish any set of acknowledgements without becoming aware of how much I owe the Research Centre for Applied Linguistics at the University of Cambridge. I learned so much of what I know about listening and spoken discourse from Gillian Brown, about cognitive approaches to language skills from John Williams and about testing from Alistair Pollitt. It is sad indeed that the centre no longer exists for the benefit of future thinkers and researchers in our field.

And finally – thanks to Paul Siedlecki, who put up with many a rambling account of what this book aimed to achieve when his mind was really full of rock formations.

John Field, London, December 2018

INTRODUCTION

Testing second language listening proficiency validly and reliably has always posed a challenge. In the days before the widespread availability of recorded material, tests were reliant upon the voice of the examiner. Each test administration was a unique phonetic event, with enormous variations of delivery between examiners and even within the performance of a single examiner on different occasions. The presentation was read-aloud, and the texts chosen were often those that had been written to be read (including literary extracts). The resulting input to test takers bore little resemblance to natural connected speech.

There were also difficulties of methodology. While accuracy in listening is critical to comprehension, it was often the only consideration. Listening was conceptualised in terms of the ability to decode speech at the phoneme or word level, with the result that perceptual processes were heavily targeted. At one point, minimal pair discrimination was employed. At another, the use of dictation with all its associated conventions (clearly enunciated clauses delivered twice, pauses for writing, instructions on punctuation) was widespread. For a comprehensive account in relation to the early Cambridge English exams, see Weir et al., 2013: 347–419.

Even with the advent of the cassette, and later the CD, problems remained. The most intractable of them was and is that the listening process takes place in the mind of the listener. Given this, how can one obtain measurable external evidence that an adequate level of understanding has been achieved? The answer was found in a method widely employed for testing reading in both first and second languages – the comprehension question. Applying this type of approach to the testing of listening was, however, not without complications. Most obviously, it engages a second skill if the questions are presented in written form, with some of the processes engaged by a test inevitably loading on to reading. Indeed, it can create what psychologists term a *divided attention* situation (Wickens, 1984, Styles 2006: 153–181), where a test taker has to handle both spoken and written text simultaneously. It also suggests false parallels between reading and listening, which do not hold up to inspection. For example, when designing reading comprehension items, one can rely on the knowledge that (thanks to spelling conventions) all words in the text appear in a standardised form and are likely to be recognised if they fall within the test taker's lexicon. This is not the case for a listening text, where words may vary considerably from their citation forms and much depends upon the way in which the material is delivered by the speaker.

The widespread use of comprehension questions in testing both reading and listening has further implications for test scoring. It is very easy for testers to lose sight of the fact they are basing their judgements on a count of correct answers rather than a construct-specific measure of listening competence. If a test taker scores 8 out of 10 in a test, the assumption is made that he/she is a competent listener at the targeted proficiency level. It is an assumption that may well be justified. But the result may tell us no more than that the test taker succeeded in extracting eight points of information from the input that corresponded to those selected by the item writer, perhaps partly by means of making strategic guesses at word or phrase level. It does not follow that he/she recognises the links between these points of information, has understood the text as a whole, or can report the intentions of the speaker.

What is more, comprehension questions come in a variety of formats (multiple-choice, gap-filling, multiple-matching, form-filling etc.), often designed with ease of marking in mind rather than the replication of a natural listening event. Most current tests do well to employ a variety of these formats rather than just one, but we tend to take for granted the construct validity of the tasks generated. They may in fact require the listener to perform rather more complex operations than those that would occur in real-world listening. In addition, there is the question of whether these formats impose a similar level of demands on the test taker. Do some entail tasks that are more challenging than others?

It is now over a decade and a half since Buck's (2001) comprehensive review of established practice in the assessing of L2 listening. The time therefore seems right to take a fresh look at the conventional listening test. The approach that is adopted here reflects recent interest among language testers in the mind of the test taker (O'Sullivan, 2011). It takes a specifically cognitive perspective; and an important underlying concern is whether the processes in which an L2 listener engages in a test environment can be said to be representative of the processes that he/she would engage in the world beyond the test.

The first part of the book attempts to lay down a set of principles which might inform the development of future listening tests. There will be two lines of attack. One recognises that the designers of tests of L2 listening (and indeed classroom practitioners) have often been insufficiently informed about the true nature of the construct that they are aiming to tackle. A model of listening is therefore proposed in Chapter 1, which systematically profiles the way in which an expert listener performs, and thus the goal towards which the second language learner is progressing. Chapter 2 begins by reviewing some principles central to the development of expertise in any skill, from rowing to playing chess. It then examines the limitations that affect most second language listening and distinguish it from more expert behaviour.

These insights, it will be argued, can form the basis for future performance descriptors that are underpinned by cognitive theory and empirical evidence. A set of sample descriptors along these lines is provided in Chapter 3. Drawing upon the Chapter 1 model, a number of areas are identified that distinguish between listener performance at the six different levels of the Common European Framework (CEFR). These, it is suggested, might add an additional set of research-supported and cognitively-based criteria to the rather underspecified CEFR descriptors.

The second section of the book (Chapters 4 to 8) adopts a different line of attack. It focuses in turn upon each of five major constituents of a typical test of L2 listening, describes how they are currently handled, and pinpoints ways in which some of these test facets potentially compromise construct validity. This leads to concrete proposals for revising some of the standard assumptions about how we should be testing the skill in L2 contexts.

In considering the content of the recorded input (Chapters 4 and 5), the emphasis is not simply on conventional considerations associated with the 'recording-as-text' (i.e. the language of the script) but also on the recording as an auditory phenomenon. There is then (Chapter 6) a review of the current conventions adopted in presenting the recorded materials and the test items to the candidate; some of these conventions, it will be suggested, can compromise the extent to which a test accurately represents real-world listening conditions. Chapter 7 explores the types of test format used in listening tests and examines their impact upon the test taker in terms of the cognitive demands that they impose. The major part of Chapter 8 then goes on to consider the ways in which test items are designed and formulated and suggests how they could be more systematically targeted in order to elicit particular responses from candidates. Extending this analysis, a brief section reflects on the extent to which a test score based upon correct answers to assorted comprehension questions can be said to measure listening proficiency with any degree of precision.

The next section of the book considers some situations where we have to adjust the assumptions that underlie mainstream tests of L2 listening. Chapter 9 examines the specific needs and characteristics of certain groups of test taker. There is first a consideration of the type of listening that an academic listener has to undertake, with suggestions as to how this information might shape test design. This is followed by an exploration of the ways in which the cognitive capabilities of young learners differ from those of adults; again, there are implications for test design. A third section briefly highlights two types of test taker whose listening needs are closely shaped by the real-world demands that they face when operating in a second language. Chapter 10 then focuses on a very different way in which the standard type of L2 listening test can be varied: it discusses the pros and cons of representing listening in terms of its interaction with the other three skills.

Chapter 11 reports on a recent study that investigated a test facet largely neglected as a factor affecting the difficulty of a recording – namely, the density of information in a text and its effect upon the listener's ability to construct a representation of what has been heard. The study explores the practicality of counting information units within a script and asks whether criteria defining a unit of information can be applied consistently by item writers. It then goes on to examine evidence of how, in practice, item writers manipulate information content in order to control test and task difficulty.

A final chapter then brings together some of the major threads that have been identified in the course of the book.

A COGNITIVE MODEL
FOR TESTING LISTENING

1 What does expert listening consist of?

The role of cognitive criteria

There has been a recent growth of interest in what goes on in the mind of a test taker and in whether these mental operations are sufficiently representative of the construct being tested (Field, 2013). The account given here suggests ways in which an understanding of the processes that contribute to the listening skill can reshape received ideas as to how the skill is best tested in second language learners. A background to this can be found in arguments put forward by Weir (2005). In presenting his Socio-Cognitive Framework, Weir makes the telling point that statistical validation after a test has taken place is not enough to ensure that the test achieves *construct validity* i.e. that it accurately and representatively measures candidates' proficiency in the skill being targeted. He emphasises the importance of ensuring that language test design is underpinned from the outset by a full understanding of the behaviour to be tested.

Put simply, the message is that, when designing a test of one of the language skills, we need extensive information about the nature of the phenomenon we are dealing with. This enables us to shape the material and tasks that we devise so as to ensure that they truly measure competence in the skill. Given that modern-day tests aspire to be tests of language performance, not simply tests of language knowledge, it is not enough to rely solely or mainly upon linguistic criteria to determine the difficulty of a test's content. Materials and tasks need to be constructed with long-term targets in mind, based on what we know of the behaviour of experienced performers of a given skill. Alongside that, a full understanding is also needed of the factors that shape the performance of novices at different stages of acquiring the skill and limit their ability to perform like an expert.

Familiarity with the cognitive processes that underlie the production and reception of language brings three major benefits to second-language test design.

a. It enables testers to provide more precise descriptors of the different levels of proficiency that are targeted by a test or a suite of tests;

b. It enables testers to target their test material more precisely, with a view to eliciting certain processes that are critical to skilled performance;

c. It directs attention to the circumstances under which language is delivered and received. It thus highlights the importance of creating materials which resemble so far as possible those that occur in real-world contexts, and formats which elicit responses representative of real-world performance.

Cognitive criteria also enable commentators to evaluate existing tests to establish how adequately and comprehensively they represent the skill being targeted. The concept of *cognitive validity* (Glaser, 1991) raises the question of whether the performance of a test taker during a test can be said to resemble the type of behaviour that would occur in a non-test situation. The concept was originally applied to testing in fields such as philosophy, medicine and science, where the issue was whether a test could be said to demonstrate that those who took it had not only mastered certain facts but had also mastered a way of thinking associated with the domain in question. Its relevance to skills-based tests of language is obvious: can we be sure that a high score in a test is indicative of the ability to handle real-world tasks that involve listening, speaking, reading or writing? The question is particularly relevant in the case of tests like IELTS, TOEFL or the British Council's Aptis test, which are used to establish whether an individual has achieved a sufficiently high level of expertise in English to accomplish particular professional or academic activities in the real world. For an extended application of the concept of cognitive validity to the testing of L2 listening, see Field 2013.

A model of expert listening

In short, a profile of how a competent listener listens is not simply a piece of interesting academic background. It can materially assist the design of L2 listening tests. It can supply a picture of the long-term goal towards which L2 listening instruction aims. It can also provide evidence-based descriptors of the components of listening that learners are expected to have mastered at different proficiency levels. Information about the processes underlying listening thus assists test designers to produce recorded materials and test items that are both sensitive to learner difficulties and systematic in focusing on aspects of the skill that constitute marks of progress.

We can, of course, already draw upon the proficiency levels of the Common European Framework of Reference for Languages or CEFR (Council of Europe, 2001). However, the CEFR criteria for listening are not as comprehensive as they might be. Though several different modes of listening are represented, the descriptors provided refer mainly to features of the input that the listener can be expected to comprehend: the topic, the linguistic content, the type of discourse and the speaker's delivery. They also refer to varying conditions of noise, which are unlikely to be a problem in a test. They thus provide at best only a rough guide to item writers, in that they do not specify very precisely the type of listening behaviour that can be expected at the various levels and how that behaviour is likely to change with growing proficiency. See Taylor (2013: 9–19) for an overview of these and other descriptors used in L2 listening tests.

Furthermore, although the CEFR descriptors are based upon the accumulated experience of distinguished ELT specialists, they are not specifically linked to what research has told us about the nature of the listening skill. This is by no means to deny the usefulness of the CEFR criteria. But we need to recognise that these days they are put to many different functions (particularly within testing) that they were not originally designed for. In developing future tests of listening, it therefore makes sense to supplement the CEFR specifications with an additional set of criteria that can both guide item writing and ensure that the grading of recordings, tasks and items takes place in a principled way. One might even potentially specify how many items within a test should aim to elicit a particular process – thus ensuring that the way in which the skill is tested will be consistent across different versions of the same test.

With these considerations in mind, there follows a brief account of the nature of skilled listening, which draws upon well-documented psycholinguistic evidence. The profile below (adapted from Field, 2008a, 2013) recognises the listening skill as falling into five distinct phases, which will be referred to as *operations*.

The downward arrows indicate a progression from smaller to larger units of language and from linguistic information based upon strings of words to more abstract representations based upon meaning. However, the upward arrows remind us that this is not a purely linear progression.

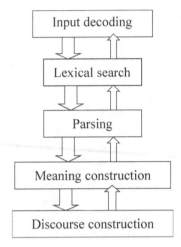

Figure 1: A simplified cognitive model of the listening process

Listening, even in L1, is very much a hit-and-miss operation which draws upon multiple cues as to which words are present. Larger units can influence the recognition of smaller ones. For example, knowledge of the spoken form of a whole word can influence perception at phoneme level. Similarly, wider context can influence what we think we hear; or (especially in the case of an L2 listener) can fill gaps in understanding or redress mishearings.

The first three operations illustrated are largely *perceptual*. Listeners have first to engage in *decoding* the input – i.e. to relate the sensations reaching their ears to the sounds of the target language. This is not as easy as it might appear. The phoneme is a highly variable unit, and its exact form depends very much on the phonemes that precede and follow it (Field, 2014a). Indeed, it has been suggested that a listener may actually analyse speech at the level of the syllable (Massaro, 1974, Mattys & Melhorn, 2005) rather than using any smaller unit.

Listeners then have to match groups of those sounds or syllables to known words. This second operation (*lexical search*) may sound easy, but is in fact very demanding because of the way in which word forms change in connected speech (Brown, 1990, Field, 2008a: 140–162, Gimson, 2008: 294–311). Speakers tend to take the easiest route when delivering speech and as a result the words they produce often diverge markedly from the kinds of citation form that are included in L2 vocabulary instruction. Examples of this appear in the panel below.

The inconsistent signal

Weak forms: *of / have* → [əv]   *a / are / of* → [ə]   *for a walk* → [frə] walk

Resyllabification: *can't help it* → (carn) tell pit   *need rain* → knee drain

Elision: *next spring* → neck spring   *East coast* → Eas coast   *isn't right* → isn right

　　　walked past → walk past

Assimilation: *ten people* → tem people   *hot bath* → hop bath

Reduction in common multi-word chunks: *do you know what I mean?* → narp mean?

　　going to → [gənə]   should have (done) → [ʃʊdə]

A second obstacle to easy recognition at word level is that words in con-nected speech are not all of the same level of prominence. Some, to be sure, carry intonational stress, marking them as important and ensuring that they are quite clearly enunciated. But the most frequent set of items in the language, the function words, are usually delivered in weak form and are downgraded in terms of loudness and duration compared to meaning-bearing content words. This is not insignificant, given that up to 50% of everyday English speech may consist of functors.

A further issue for the listener is that there are no consistent spaces between words as there are in written texts. The listener is presented with a string of syllables and has to work out where, within that string, one word ends and the next begins – a process known as *lexical segmentation*. The result of all this is that listening, even in one's first language, is quite a tentative process, with a listener forming an immediate impression of what has been heard, which may have to be revised. Sometimes a word is not fully recognised until two or three words later (Grosjean, 1985).

Even when a word's form has been accurately identified, there may be further problems in retrieving the intended meaning. Many words have not one but a range of senses which vary according to the co-text that accompanies them. Compare the word RUN in *run a mile, run a bath, run a business, run an idea past somebody.* The listener may have to hold all these possible senses in reserve until the whole utterance has been heard and the correct one can be chosen.

At a third stage, the listener has to assemble a group of words into a syntactic pattern – an operation known as *parsing.* It is important to real-ise that this entails holding in the mind all the words that have been identified so far in a given group, until such time as the listener can trace a pattern in them (e.g. a Subject-Verb-Object sequence). This may not happen until the speaker gets to the end of an utterance and pauses briefly to plan the next one. Because the message is being processed word by word, the listener sometimes develops expectations about how it is likely to develop (Tanenhaus & Trueswell, 1995). For example, hearing *The policeman accused...*, a listener might anticipate the words *...the suspect*; and would then have to rapidly revise this assumption if the words turned out to be *...of bribery*. Here is a further illustration of how, even in L1, listening is necessarily tentative because it takes place in real time.

Following parsing, the linguistic form of the signal is converted into a unit of information. The next two operations involve handling this information and are therefore sometimes described as 'conceptual' because language is no longer involved. The information obtained is at first without any context and, during *meaning construction,* it has to be enriched by drawing upon the listener's world knowledge, knowledge of the speaker and recall of the current topic of conversation. It might have to be interpreted in relation to the speaker's apparent intentions. It may also be necessary to infer ideas that the speaker has not explicitly expressed and to interpret back-referring anaphors such as pronouns (*she, they, it, this*).

Then, at a final stage (*discourse construction*), the new piece of information has to be added to what the listener has understood of the exchange so far. Its relative importance has to be established, it has to be connected to previous pieces of information, and it has to be integrated into the overall line of argument presented by the speaker[1].

So how can this model assist testers to design more targeted tests of listening? Well, firstly, it provides a five-stage framework for designing descriptors that indicate what can be expected of learners at different proficiency levels. Secondly, within each of the operations identified, there are sets of well authenticated processes which are critical to successful listening. These are quite distinct from the 'sub-skills' of yore (Richards, 1983), which were useful in focusing attention on the component parts of the skill but were mainly intuitive. Instead, they are mental processes that

---

[1] The distinction between these last two levels is not always fully represented in psycholinguistic models of listening (e.g. in the model proposed by Cutler & Clifton, 1999); however, it is very much part of the view of comprehension taken by discourse analysts such as Brown & Yule, 1983.

have been investigated by researchers and shown to be psychologically real. Examples (taken from Field, 2008a) appear in Appendix A of this volume; but, to give a flavour, processes at word recognition level might include:

- building syllables into words;
- using the stressed syllable of a word as a cue to its identity;
- using the word that bears intonation stress to identify current topic;
- recognising words that occur in reduced form;
- recognising groups of words that often occur together;
- identifying in connected speech where one word ends and the next begins;
- mapping from the form of a word to its range of meanings.

In teaching contexts, processes of this kind can provide the basis for more focused classroom listening practice than is usually afforded by the conventional recording-plus-comprehension-questions (Field, 2008a). In testing contexts, they serve to identify important components of listening development that can inform the descriptors used to distinguish the various proficiency levels. They also potentially provide a basis for developing test items that target specific aspects of the skill that form part of a learner's developing competence (See Chapter 8).

2 The second language listener

The operations displayed in Figure 1 are those employed by an expert listener; they may obviously be modified or absent in the performance of listeners who are less skilled. In the case of those listening to a second language, two general factors limit their performance: one being level of *knowledge* (linguistic or cultural) and the other level of *expertise*. Their consequence is that, for many listeners, the L2 listening experience differs markedly from the L1 listening one, with likely failures of decoding and a greater reliance upon remedial *strategies*. A further strand in the repertoire of a competently performing listener must therefore be whether he/she is capable of using strategies effectively to compensate for gaps in understanding.

Language-related knowledge

Most obviously, L2 listeners may not succeed in decoding all that is said because of limitations in their linguistic knowledge.

Phonological knowledge

Where learners possess uncertain L2 phonological values, the effect is to reduce their confidence in their ability to match acoustic input to phonemes and syllables. As a result, they may fall back on approximate matches at word level, supported by a degree of guessing based upon general context (Field, 2004).

Lexical knowledge

This is not simply a matter of the size of the vocabulary that a learner has been taught. Contrary to what some language test specifications assume, it is not enough to 'know' a word. The learner also has to *identify* it when it occurs in connected speech. As we have seen, this entails the ability to recognise the word in a number of variant forms, determined by the co-text within which the word occurs and by how precise the articulation of the speaker is. It also entails being able to divide a piece of connected speech into the words within it, which may not be easy since the way in which word boundaries are indicated varies from one language to another.

In terms of meaning, an L2 listener may have to learn to associate not a single sense with a word form but a range of senses that depend upon the word's co-text. Compare, for example, the different interpretations of the phonological form /raɪt/ in sequences such as: ... *turn* / ... *in front of you* / *you're quite* ... / ... *a letter*.). As experience of listening to a second language increases, a learner also acquires the ability to recognise larger units in the form of commonly occurring chunks of language (Wray, 2001). This helps to resolve ambiguities at word level and assists the listener in identifying function words of low prominence.

Grammatical knowledge

Across a group of words (usually a clause), L2 listeners draw upon their stored knowledge of grammar, which directs their attention to such features as syntactic structure, inflections or auxiliary verbs. However, 'knowing' a point of grammar is by no means the same as identifying an example of it in the speech of somebody else and associating that example, not with a rule but with the semantics that underlie it. It is of little use for a listener to interpret *I should have phoned her* in terms of 'modal + perfect participle'; what is required is a recognition that 'should have done' relates to an unfulfilled action and is likely (in functional terms) to be an expression of regret.

On top of this, since speech reaches the ears a syllable at a time, a listener has to build up a syntactic structure in the mind little by little. Here, parsing is helped by factors such as an understanding of how strongly the target language relies on word order (Bates & MacWhinney, 1989). English has a relatively consistent Subject-Verb-Object order which assists listeners in parsing, whereas other languages show more flexibility.

Finally, it is worth noting that even basic verb forms in English are not as easy to decode as commentators sometimes assume. Markers of tense and aspect in English are often of low prominence and difficult to identify. So indeed are the function words which potentially provide valuable cues to syntactic structure (Field, 2008b).

Cultural knowledge

Obviously, there is a distinct possibility that the expectations that L2 learners bring to a listening encounter will be shaped by their own background and by an incomplete understanding of the background of the speaker. But perhaps the most important cultural factor so far as comprehension is concerned lies in the forms of language that a speaker uses. How familiar is an L2 listener with the pragmatics of the second language (the forms of words used to offer, apologise, invite, suggest) in order to interpret the speaker's underlying intentions? How familiar is the listener with the markers of style that indicate a speaker's attitude to the listener and to the topic (polite, non-committal, ironic, bored, anxious)? Attitude in particular may be conveyed not simply by the form of words used, but also by intonation patterns peculiar to the second language.

Expertise in handling connected speech

While language knowledge is clearly important, the effectiveness with which it is employed depends critically upon how *accessible* the information is to the user and how *automatic* is the connection made between what is heard and the corresponding linguistic units.

An obvious example can be found in how vocabulary is processed. An L2 listener first encounters problems of recognition in the form of the many variant forms that words may take in connected speech. Once a word has been confidently identified, there is then a complex process of *mapping* from the spoken form to a set of information stored in the mind, which includes the word's range of senses and its grammatical function. In novice listeners, this process is inevitably slow and uncertain – partly because of limited spoken-word vocabulary, partly because of uncertainty about how accurate their word recognition has been – but also (importantly) because of a lack of practice in achieving the mapping process in relation to L2 words. It can take some considerable time before L2 learners have had sufficient experience for the links between words and their meanings to have become automatic.

Something similar is true of syntactic parsing. As already noted, generalised knowledge of grammar rules is of little assistance to the listener unless it is supported by a mastery of the processes for applying the rules to incoming speech. These processes require the listener first to build up a grammatical structure word by word and then to map automatically from the structure to the concepts that it represents.

The importance of *automaticity* in these and other processes is paramount. If a basic operation like matching a set of speech sounds to a word requires an effort of attention, it imposes demands upon a listener's working memory that can restrict wider thought processes (Gathercole & Baddeley, 1993). Because of their language limitations and because of their inexperience in listening to the target language, early L2 learners have to dedicate large resources of attention to input decoding, lexical search and parsing. So long as this is the case, they have insufficient attention free for handling higher-level operations like making inferences, interpreting a speaker's intentions, recognising a line of argument and so on (Field 2013: 106–7). Extensive evidence from learner transcription (see the typical example in Figure 2) suggests that a perceptible threshold is reached just before CEFR B2 level, when processing at lexical level becomes markedly more accurate and more automatic. The effect of this is to free up attention, enabling learners to report on deeper and more global aspects of meaning.

Automaticity also affects how much language can be stored temporarily in the mind in order to trace a grammatical pattern in it. Lower proficiency learners having to focus a lot of attention on identifying words

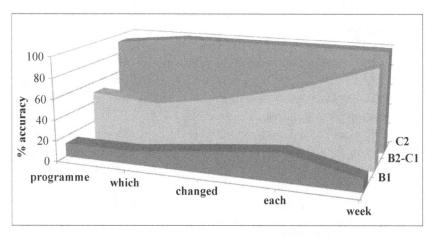

Figure. 2: Percentage of learners accurately reporting words in authentic connected speech: three different proficiency levels (N=20 in each)
(Field, 2008a: 290)

in connected speech find themselves without enough memory capacity to retain more than a few of those words. As word recognition becomes more automatic and demands less and less effort, learners become capable of holding on to longer utterances.

In a parallel development already mentioned, L2 listeners around B1+ level come to recognise commonly occurring groups of words and to use them in effect as units of vocabulary (Wray, 2001). Storing a single familiar chunk in the mind obviously makes parsing easier than storing words one by one.

Strategic competence

Using strategies effectively is an important component in an early-stage L2 listener's struggle after meaning (Field, 2008a: 286–303). Note that the strategies referred to here are solely communication strategies (Cohen's (1998) 'strategies of use'), not strategies for learning language or test-wise strategies (Field, 2012a) that exploit the weaknesses of a test format. In discussing listening, they can be viewed as *compensatory* in purpose: the test taker using a degree of guesswork to fill in gaps where parts of the input have not been accurately matched to words. There has been considerable research interest in this type of listening strategy (see Macaro, Graham & Vanderplank, 2007 for a review). Those who have proposed taxonomies of them include Rost (1990:177), Field (2008a: 293–302), Lynch (2009:80) and Vandergrift (1997).

The judicious use of strategies of this kind can extend the comprehension of a listener well beyond what their knowledge and expertise might otherwise permit. Strategic competence should therefore be seen by testers as an important component of L2 listening proficiency, as Canale & Swain (1980) suggest. The ability to identify the general meaning of a text, even where much of the wording has not been accurately decoded, should arguably feature in listening descriptors, especially at levels A1 to B1. To be sure, strategy use may often be restricted at the very lowest levels, where difficulties of decoding can result in a lack of reliably-identified words and phrases on which to base hypotheses. But the value of being able to extract the topic or main point from a piece of speech should nonetheless be recognised at these levels, and rewarded as an important part of real-world listening competence.

Once decoding and lexical search become more proficient, strategy use is less critical to understanding; but listeners continue to rely to some extent upon approaching L2 input strategically. The characteristics of competent higher-level strategy use include an awareness of not one but several strategic solutions to a problem of understanding and the ability to choose between them. For example, confronted with an unfamiliar word, a listener should be capable of deciding whether it is a known one produced in a non-standard form or a new one. If the latter, they should be able to decide between ignoring the word as not important to the wider picture, gaining a general sense of the word's meaning or using morphology, co-text and/or context to attach a more precise meaning. What this illustrates for the test designer is the need, just occasionally, to relax control over the language of the recording, in order to ensure that it contains words or expressions that are *beyond* what one might expect the test taker to know.

3 Performance at different proficiency levels

Tests of second language performance fall into two distinct types:
- those that test learners using material that targets a *specific level of proficiency* (maybe forming part of a suite of tests at different levels). The results determine whether a test taker has succeeded or failed at this level.
- those that test learners with material that *covers a range of levels*, in order to determine at what point they cease to be able to perform consistently. The results thus attribute a level of proficiency to the test taker.

In either case, it is critical for test designers to have clear and comprehensive descriptors that specify the type of performance that can be expected of candidates at different levels of competence. The remarks that follow and the recommendations made have relevance to both types of situation.

Criteria for listening descriptors

When designing specifications for listening materials, test providers and materials writers often choose to represent the processes to be targeted in terms of very broad 'listening for' categories such as 'listening for gist', 'listening for main point', 'listening for information' etc. The problem with these 'listening for' categories is that they have remained poorly defined. There are uncertain boundaries between 'listening for gist', 'listening for main point' and 'listening for global meaning' or 'listening for facts', 'listening for information' and 'listening for scanning' or 'listening for local information' and 'listening for detail'. In addition, there has been little discussion about precisely what elements of the listening construct such general listening types elicit from the test taker and how representative they are of the skill as a whole. As a result, they are rarely, if ever, linked to different levels of L2 listening development or graded in terms of their relative difficulty. A further issue is that the 'listening for' categories constitute rather arbitrary goals that, in the real world, are very much determined by the nature of the communication that is taking place and by the listener's own decisions about what he/she wants to extract from it.

A widely adopted alternative is to match the general goals of a test against the criteria that the Common European Framework uses to characterise each of its proficiency levels. However, as noted, these descriptors are quite limited, especially at the lowest and highest levels. They make use of relative terms such as *quite, very* etc and occasionally relate to circumstances such as ambient noise which are not relevant to the testing situation. The fact is that neither approach to categorising listening has so far provided us with detailed descriptors that are sufficiently representative of what psycholinguistic research and theory have told us about the listening construct.

A case can therefore be made for considerably amplifying the descriptors that are currently used to guide item writers and to inform stakeholders about test content. In Chapter 1, the suggestion was made that an approach to describing L2 listening development might draw upon research evidence of how expert listeners behave. Treating the behaviour of an expert listener as the end-point towards which L2 listening instruction must aim enables us to identify a complete set of processes to be acquired. These can then be matched against what a learner is capable of at various levels of proficiency. Chapter 2 then went on to provide a profile of the L2 listener which considered the constraints that affect performance while a learner is in the course of achieving proficiency. Briefly, four factors were identified in the earlier discussion as making a contribution to overall competence.

- *Knowledge of language.* Linguistic criteria in the form of lists of vocabulary and grammatical structures feature quite prominently in the handbooks produced by exam providers for the information of teachers and other stakeholders. However, in the case of listening, consideration should also be given to the perceptual difficulties involved. In terms of vocabulary, language needs to be represented, not just as simple knowledge of spoken word citation forms but also as the ability to *recognise* those words when they occur (sometimes in quite degraded forms) in connected speech. In terms of grammar, it needs to be represented as the ability to assemble a syntactic structure, bearing in mind that the relevant information reaches the ears word by word.
- *Cultural knowledge.* Descriptors should represent the extent to which learners are able to interpret a speaker's intentions in relation to pragmatics (suggesting, offering, apologising etc) and in relation to markers of style (politeness, neutrality, concern etc.).

Both may depend upon the listener's ability to interpret not just the words used but the intonation patterns that are characteristic of the target language.

- *Expertise.* Descriptors should represent a progressive develop-ment in an L2 listener's ability to deploy the fundamental pro-cesses that make up competent listening. Two factors particularly deserve consideration:

    - how *automatic* a learner's L2 listening processes have become. Automaticity deserves to be a criterion in any set of descriptors of L2 listening, given that it marks a consider-able breakthrough in processing ability between a learner at B1 level and one at B2. It has implications for the listener's ability to move on from low-level processes such as recog-nising words to interpreting the meanings that the speaker intends to convey and building a record of the line of argu-ment that the speaker develops. Of course, as the concept of automaticity is not widely recognised in ELT contexts, it makes sense, when designing descriptors for stakeholders or item writers, to represent it in more concrete terms. One way is to refer to the observable outcomes of automatic process-ing, in the form of greater *accuracy* of word recognition and greater *speed of response* to an interlocutor.

    - The recognition of recurrent *chunks of language* which, stored as if they were vocabulary items, reduce some of the effort of word-by-word parsing.

- *Strategic competence.* Descriptors should specify how success-ful the early-stage listener is in compensating for the patchy and approximate way in which the input from the speaker is received, due to problems of input decoding and word recogni-tion. At higher levels, the focus might be on the ability to handle unfamiliar lexical items.

Towards cognitively based descriptors of L2 listening

Mention has been made of the marked shift in the scope of the listening processes available to a learner which occurs between CEFR levels B1 and B2. In any test, whether level-specific or cross-level, it makes good sense to use this watershed as a central point around which performance descriptors can be constructed. The implications are that:

- At proficiency levels below CEFR B1+, the main focus in any descriptors should be on *perceptual processes* and on the test taker's gradually increasing ability to handle them automatically (i.e. rapidly, accurately and with minimal effort).
- At proficiency levels below CEFR B1+, descriptors should include mention of the *strategic competence* of the learners, which may be a critical means of resolving gaps in understanding.
- At proficiency levels of B2 and above, the focus in any descriptors should be on *meaning-based processes* and on the learner's increasing ability to handle meaning construction and discourse construction.

The descriptors that follow are designed to be of use in both test design and item writing, supplementing the sometimes meagre CEFR criteria. Technical terms have been avoided to ensure that item writers can follow the criteria.

Perceptual processing

Let us begin by considering in detail what a learner can be expected to be capable of achieving at CEFR level B2 strictly in terms of *perceptual processing*. The corresponding CEFR descriptors are quoted first by way of reference.

CEFR perceptual criteria for Level B2

Can understand standard spoken language, live or broadcast, on both familiar and unfamiliar topics normally encountered in personal, social, academic or vocational life. Only extreme background noise, inadequate discourse structure and/or idiomatic usage influences the ability to understand.

B2 Level: perceptual performance

Shows signs of the ability to process spoken input rapidly and generally accurately – overcoming the challenges posed by reduced word forms and variations in word prominence.

- Accurately identifies most familiar content words in connected speech, regardless of their prominence.
- Accurately identifies closed-class words of low prominence and the functions they are performing.
- Is proficient at segmenting connected speech into words.
- Shows signs of processing groups of words in chunks.
- Rapidly and accurately matches word forms to their meanings – as manifested in the speed and accuracy of responses to an interlocutor.
- Recognises recurrent chunks of language in connected speech and may reproduce them in replies.
- Is able to retain long sections of spoken language in working memory in order to parse them.
- Is able to distinguish new words from known ones, and to make reasoned judgements as to the meanings of the new words.
- Shows quite a sound understanding of speaker intentions, as conveyed by pragmatics and by the content of what is said.

Tracking backwards from this threshold point enables us to characterise the more limited range of processes used by learners from A1 up to B1 levels. Each of the profiles that follows draws upon the cognitive criteria discussed previously as well as the author's own experience of working with listeners at a range of levels; and is further supported by evidence from paused transcription (Field, 2008c). Note that the focus is strictly on the behaviour of the test taker; future chapters will consider the way in which the input and the tasks that are chosen might reflect the proficiency level being targeted.

CEFR perceptual criterion for Level A1

Can follow speech which is very slow and clearly articulated, with long pauses for him/her to assimilate meaning.

A1 Level performance

Can identify isolated words that provide relevant information. Ability to follow L2 speech is limited to very simple points of information (times, prices, spellings, basic adjectives and prepositions of position). May be able to handle short instructions and descriptions.

- Recognises a limited set of frequent and familiar words (numbers, colours, alphabet used to spell out words) if they are close to their citation forms.
- Is unable to identify many function words.
- Misunderstandings result from incorrect identification of prominent words.
- Matching words to their meanings is effortful, as reflected in hesitant and inaccurate replies to speakers.
- Relies heavily on decoding at word level.
- Can infer some very limited factual information (usually based on single words), despite large gaps in understanding.
- Can sometimes guess the main point of a text.
- Strategy use is limited to very approximate matches between unfamiliar words and known ones.

CEFR criteria for Level A2

Can understand phrases and expressions related to areas of most immediate priority (e.g. very basic personal and family information, shopping, local geography, employment) provided speech is clearly and slowly articulated.

A2 Level performance

Can handle simple text types that are sequential (narration/description/instruction).

- Recognises frequent and familiar content words.
- Is often not accurate in identifying function words and recognising their contribution to meaning.
- Is quite reliant on decoding at word level.
- Some misunderstandings occur due to incorrect identification of prominent words.
- Matching words to their meanings is effortful; slow to supply answers to speaker questions.
- Can hold short simple clauses in the mind for the purposes of parsing.
- Can state the main point of a text in general terms.
- Shows signs of strategy use – mainly by using prominent words in order to guess wider factual meanings.
- Understanding of speaker intentions is limited to the transmission of facts.

CEFR perceptual criteria for Level B1

Can understand straightforward factual information about common everyday or job-related topics, identifying both general messages and specific details, provided speech is clearly articulated in a generally familiar accent. Can understand the main points of clear standard speech on familiar matters regularly encountered in work, school, leisure etc., including short narratives.

B1 Level performance

Can handle text types that are sequential – including expositions with a clear line of development. But continues to process information as loosely connected facts.

- Recognises quite a large proportion of prominent content words, but there are residual problems of word recognition.
- Identifies common function words and recognises their contribution to meaning.
- Some misunderstandings remain from misidentifying prominent words.
- Often successful in segmenting connected speech into words.
- Matching words to their meanings is sometimes slow, especially with homonyms and polysemous words.
- Shows early signs of processing groups of words in chunks; but retains a focus on word-level information.
- Can hold simple clauses of around six words in the mind for parsing.
- Can infer factual information, despite gaps in understanding.
- Can state the main point of a text quite accurately.
- Engages in strategy use: constructing contexts around recognised words.
- Understands speaker intentions expressed in terms of very basic functions.

Processing for meaning

Chapter 2 traced an inverse relationship between the amount of attention that an L2 listener needs to give to perceptual processing at word and clause level and his/her ability to focus on wider issues relating to the interpretation and organisation of what has been heard. Accordingly, the descriptors proposed above for lower levels focused principally on perceptual processes. On a similar line of reasoning, we can take it for granted that test takers at Level B2 and beyond have largely mastered the processes involved in lexical search and parsing. If there are problems at word and clause level, they are likely to reflect gaps in language knowledge as the demands of vocabulary and grammar increase, rather than inadequate listening expertise. What must chiefly distinguish listeners at higher proficiency levels, therefore, is their relative ability to handle the information that they have succeeded in extracting. The panel below identifies what one might expect to characterise test taker behaviour at B2 level. Note that it draws mainly on what was referred to earlier as *meaning construction* – i.e. on the ways in which a listener interprets and elaborates on pieces of information as they are received. The profile is preceded by the relevant CEFR descriptors.

CEFR meaning-based criteria for Level B2

Can understand the main topics of propositionally and linguistically complex speech on both concrete and abstract topics delivered in a standard dialect, including technical discussions in his/her field of specialisation.

Can follow extended speech and complex lines of argument, provided the topic is reasonably familiar and the direction of the talk is signposted by explicit markers.

B2 Level: meaning-based performance

Can handle expository and discursive texts with clear connectives.

- Can identify and report most points in a 3–4 minute recording.
- Is aware of the general line of argument that links these points.
- Is capable of placing a speaker's comments in a wider context.
- Employs world knowledge and knowledge of the topic, context, speaker etc to enrich understanding.
- Can infer some meanings that have been left unstated by the speaker.
- Can infer some links between adjoining sentences, even where there are no connectives.
- Checks consistency with what was said previously.
- Can identify general speaker purpose using pragmatic and discourse signals.
- Strategy use includes inferring the sense of unfamiliar words from context – forming and checking hypotheses about unclear passages – anticipating what a speaker will cover.

Differences in the ability of lower proficiency learners to operate perceptually can be investigated by means of hard evidence in the form of constructed item responses, transcriptions and verbal reports. Processing at meaning level is more dependent upon observer interpretation; and it is therefore rather harder to differentiate categorically between the performance of L2 test takers at the C levels and those at B2. One can assume that the ability to engage world knowledge, contextualise information, form inferences and interpret speaker attitude is, in the main, sharper and more consistently reliable at C levels than at B2. But the most important area of distinction seems likely to lie in an enhanced ability to operate at discourse rather than local level. In a C level test taker, one might reasonably expect evidence of ability to:

- give attention to wider issues of meaning and to identifying lines of argument;
- distinguish main points from subsidiary ones and report the links between them;
- evaluate the points made by a speaker for their consistency and logical coherence;
- process relatively dense information.

These are the products of ever-increasing automaticity in relation to the basic listening processes. In addition, given the likely increase in the conceptual complexity of the recordings used, it remains relevant to feature one or more items which require the listener to identify the speaker's main point.

The following criteria are tentatively proposed:

CEFR criteria for Level C1

Can understand standard spoken language, live or broadcast, on both familiar and unfamiliar topics normally encountered in personal, social, academic or vocational life.

Can understand the main topics of propositionally and linguistically complex speech on both concrete and abstract topics delivered in a standard dialect, including technical discussions in his/her field of specialisation.

Can follow extended speech and complex lines of argument, provided the topic is reasonably familiar and the direction of the talk is signposted by explicit markers.

C1 Level performance

Can handle text types with quite a complex line of argument – including process-description, exposition, discussion, analysis and persuasion.
- Processes text at clause level with few or no problems of understanding.
- Can report both factual information and ideas, in some detail.
- Recognises the speaker's attitude and reports it accurately.
- Can decide the relative importance of points of information.
- Can distinguish main points from supporting detail and construct a line of argument.
- Can evaluate speaker's arguments.
- Infers unfamiliar word meanings as a matter of course.

CEFR criteria for Level C2

Has no difficulty in understanding any kind of spoken language, whether live or broadcast, delivered at fast native speed.

C2 Level performance

Can handle text types with complex lines of argument – including exposition, discussion, analysis and persuasion.
- Can report factual information in detail, clearly representing logical links between the points.
- Can report quite complex lines of argument and link them to concrete examples and applications.
- Recognises the speaker's attitude and can judge its appropriacy.
- Recognises indicators of style and formality, including implied meanings (e.g. irony).
- Can distinguish major and minor points and report their relevance to the overall discourse structure.
- Can critically evaluate a speaker's arguments and identify loopholes or omissions.

Items and recorded material can also take full advantage of the fact that at C levels listeners should be capable of processing speech that is informationally dense and where there are relatively complex links between the various points of information. However, this is not quite the same as what is sometimes vaguely referred to in test descriptors as 'abstractness' (see discussion of abtractness and imagery, pp. 48–49).

RECORDED CONTENT

4 Recording as text

In this chapter and those that follow, a number of aspects of current listening test design that we tend to take for granted will be examined critically, with particular consideration given to the way in which they shape the behaviour of the test taker. Some problematic characteristics of present-day listening tests will be identified; and concrete proposals will be made for rethinking the assumptions that underlie them. Due account will be taken of how appropriate they might or might not be at different levels of proficiency.

Let us begin, appropriately enough, with the recorded material. This chapter and the next focus on two different aspects of the spoken input used in listening tests: first, the content of the script from which the recording is generated ('recording-as-text') and then the nature of the recording as an auditory phenomenon ('recording-as-speech'). Three major questions will arise in these chapters.

- Is the language and topic content of the recordings appropriately matched to different proficiency levels?
- Are the demands of the spoken input appropriately matched to different proficiency levels?
- How representative is the material of the type of speech which the test taker is likely to encounter in real-world listening events?

The criteria provided in test handbooks and item writer instructions suggest that test providers give much more thought to the first of these than to the second and third.

The present section covers the parts played by language, text length, topic, abstractness and discourse type. It then goes on to consider other factors that are less often mentioned by commentators.

Language

General comments

Specifications for listening tests in handbooks and item writer guidelines tend to rely heavily on lists which outline the grammatical structures and vocabulary to be used. In a suite like the Cambridge English one, the purpose is to distinguish clearly between tests aimed at different stages of proficiency. In more broadly-based tests such as Aptis, language criteria are used to demonstrate the way in which a single paper manages to cover not one but a range of proficiency levels.

Clearly, guidelines are important if we are to ensure that the recorded input on which learners are assessed contains language that they can be expected to know. However, too narrow a reliance upon this kind of prescription can be counter-productive. The reason is partly that it creates the assumption that there is such a thing as a generic English language syllabus, widely shared across countries and educational cultures. But it is also because listening is a much more tentative process than reading. Listeners may encounter words that fall within their vocabulary range or grammar structures that they have studied, but fail to recognise them when they occur in connected speech.

What is more, if a test aims to predict performance in contexts beyond the test centre, it needs to make due allowance for the fact that real-world input to the listener is bound to include vocabulary and grammar which is ungraded and unfamiliar. Alongside general proficiency, a test designer needs to recognise the importance of strategic listening competence. This should occasionally license the use of material that requires a test taker to construct a provisional meaning on the basis of a partially-understood piece of text and then check the hypothesis against what comes next.

Vocabulary

The preceding comments have special resonance for how vocabulary is handled in the testing of listening. There is a long history of discussion about its role in tests of reading; but it has only recently been recognised that listening represents a different and more challenging set of circumstances. Among the issues to be considered are: How can test specifications best represent the listening vocabulary at a given proficiency level? Are the vocabulary needs of listening and reading necessarily the same? How many unknown words can we allow in a listening test without severely compromising understanding? Unfortunately, the solutions proposed by researchers often raise as many new questions as they do answers.

It has become conventional to specify the vocabulary at a given proficiency level in terms of the frequency of the items that the candidate is assumed to know. The measure is often expressed in terms of 1K (words within the most frequent thousand), 2K (words within the most frequent two thousand) and so on. There appears to be quite wide agreement

(Staehr, 2008, Milton 2009: 54) that around 2000 words (the first 2K) enable basic communication and understanding across all four language skills. So far, so good. But potential problems arise when item writers try to apply these criteria too prescriptively.

One assumption made is that frequency bands reflect the way in which vocabulary is introduced in standard coursebooks – which is by no means the case. Coursebook vocabulary tends to be structured around lexical sets (beginning with family relationships, furniture, colours, etc.) and, though it draws upon the most frequent and available items within these sets, they by no means correspond narrowly to frequency bands. A notorious example is the days of the week, which vary widely in the frequency of their use (Martin, 1988).

A second fallacy is the notion that a count derived from a corpus is a reliable indicator of the actual frequency of a piece of vocabulary and thus the extent to which it is likely to occur in natural speech. Both the BNC (British National Corpus) and the COCA (Corpus of Contemporary American English) classify spoken and written words by their *forms*; that, after all, is what a computer does well. They do not take account of homophones or indeed of the fact that the precise sense attached to an item may vary according to context and collocation (consider *heavy* in *a heavy smoker*). An incident that occurred during a recent development of pilot materials neatly illustrates this. Concerns were raised by the test provider about the word *dark* (in the context of *dark hair*) on the grounds that it did not fall into the frequency range specified for the level. The suggested substitute was *fair*, which showed up as much more frequent in the corpus consulted. However, when a rough sample was taken of a hundred occurrences of *fair* in the BNC speech corpus, only 4% of instances related to hair colour, with the vast majority carrying the sense of 'just' (48%) or 'reasonable' (16%). Far from being a more accessible option, *fair* in this sense was actually of low frequency and more likely than *dark* to be misunderstood because of the availability of a more fre-quent but inappropriate meaning (not to mention a homophone in *fare*).

In addition, we cannot determine the lexical demands of a listening pas-sage without taking account of the medium of transmission. As already noted, listening relies upon a transitory signal, in which some words are given much more prominence than others. The irony is that it is the most frequent group of words in the lexicon (namely the function words) which are consistently the least salient in natural speech because of their weak forms and short duration (Field 2008b). Word length does, incidentally, make quite an important contribution to the ease with words are recognised. Transcription evidence (Field, 2008a: 290) shows that a four-syllable word like *entertainment* is more easily identified than other shorter ones which may be of a higher frequency.

The conclusion to be drawn is that frequency bands can, at best, serve as rough indicators. When composing texts, writers do well to exhibit a degree of flexibility in the way in which word frequency targets are observed. At lower proficiency levels, lists of lexical sets may well be more useful.

A second issue that needs consideration is the relationship between receptive and productive vocabulary. The received idea is that words are generally acquired receptively and then used productively. This is indeed likely to be the case with reading and writing. However, in the case of oral vocabulary, a great deal may depend upon the learning context. In an ESL (English as a Second Language) situation, where learners are widely exposed to spoken English, transfer from receptive to productive may be indeed the principal model. But in an EFL situation, much early vocabulary will have been acquired from a teacher, with the words presented in their citation forms. When an early-stage learner comes to encounter those same words in connected speech, they will be much less easy to recognise: they may well be reduced in form and the boundaries between them will not be marked. So, in the case of listening, test designers should not assume that receptive oral vocabulary will necessarily run ahead of productive. Function words are a case in point (see the discussion above). Though they are likely to be present in quite large numbers in the speech productions of L2 learners, it may be some time before those same learners succeed consistently in identifying them in connected speech. Transcription data (Field 2008b) indicates that lower proficiency listeners focus heavily on the more prominent content words.

This brings us to the question of whether a learner's listening vocabulary is likely to be similar in size to the reading one. There might, for example, be differences due to the fact that much spoken communication is informal and relates to the here-and-now. Listeners might also sometimes be assisted by the information provided by a speaker's gestures and facial expressions, reducing their dependence on the actual words that are uttered. Then of course there is also the fact that in listening the input is transitory, so that word-matching is necessarily more approximate.

Recent research has suggested that, even in the early stages of L2 acqui-sition, knowledge of the spoken forms of words lags behind that of the written forms; and that the gap between the two becomes wider as learners become more proficient. Strikingly, Milton and Hopkins (2006) found evidence to this effect among a large group of Greek learners of English, who one might have expected to be slower to acquire written vocabulary because of the unfamiliar alphabet. Milton (2009: 183) sug-gests that a target spoken vocabulary at B2 level may be around 3000 to 3500 words and at C2 about 4500, as compared with suggestions from commentators such as Nation (2001) that the base for reading may be around 6000 or more.

Milton (2009: 179) partly attributes lower vocabulary needs in listening to the different content of written and spoken texts: 'Because reading and writing depend upon the learner's ability to handle proportionately large volumes of infrequent vocabulary, the relationship between read-ing and writing skills and vocabulary size appears relatively simple: the more words you know, the better you are likely to do. Skills that involve aural interaction may not behave this way and there may be a ceiling in vocabulary knowledge after which significant improvement in vocabu-lary scores may not be reflected in test performance'.

A final question concerns what is known as *coverage* – the relation-ship between familiar and unfamiliar vocabulary in a text. How many unknown words is it reasonable for a test designer to include in a lis-tening passage without compromising the test taker's ability to make sense of it? Researchers investigating reading have suggested that a figure of around 95% (Laufer, 1989) or 98% (Nation, 2001: 147) is a reliable target. These figures are general indications but they sometimes get cited quite categorically so it is important to understand their limita-tions. Firstly, 'comprehension' is conceived here purely in terms of cor-rect answers to factual questions, without allowing for the varying task demands that a test taker might have to meet. A reader or listener asked to report the main point of a text is arguably less likely to be fazed by unknown vocabulary than one who has to extract ten pieces of informa-tion from it. Similarly, the figures might well vary with different text con-tent (e.g. narrative versus discursive) or different styles (formal versus informal); and they do not allow for the fact that some learners are more strategic than others and thus more capable of inferring the meanings of unknown words from context.

It is also worth noting that 'coverage' figures tend to mask the relationship between content and function words. Minimally informative function words make up a large proportion of any text: McCarthy & Carter
(1997) calculate that the 50 most frequent words of English (of which 45
are function words) account for up to 48.5% of all word tokens in their
spoken corpus. So, leaving aside the other concerns, the figure of 98%
coverage may not be wide of the mark as a guideline for item writers.
It means that, in a test designed for a particular proficiency level, up to
4% of the content words included might fall outside the range of what
one would expect a test taker to know. In a typical three-minute listening
passage, that might mean around 12 words out of a total of 600. Perhaps
on the low side for a real-world situation but surely just about sufficient
to emulate, in a small way, circumstances where a listener cannot count
on every word being controlled for frequency and thus has to rely on
strategy use.

In the light of the points just made, it is interesting to ask whether recent
thinking on vocabulary knowledge is reflected in the intuitive practice of
experienced item writers. How constrained are item writers by considerations of frequency and by the need to limit the use of unknown vocabulary? Table 1 provides an example of actual patterns of vocabulary
selection for listening, showing the range of frequency bands up to K10
across sample listening papers at five levels of the Cambridge English
suite (from KET targeting CEFR level A2 to CPE targeting CEFR Level
C2). At all proficiency levels, there is a heavy weighting towards K1
and K2 vocabulary – unavoidably, given the high frequency of function
words. An occasional word above K6 occurs; but, at the top two levels,
one has to assume that the additional demands imposed by the listening
script derive largely from the complexity of ideas expressed and the links
between them, rather than from the use of esoteric words.

Test/freq.	K1	K2	K3	K4	K5	K6–10
KET	93.72	3.53	0.74	0.2	0.29	0.22
PET	92.38	4.64	1.16	0.43	0.36	0.22
FCE	90.23	5.6	1.53	0.68	0.39	0.53
CAE	87.43	6.05	2.36	1.3	0.63	0.92
CPE	86.94	5.36	2.5	1.16	0.79	1.48

**Table 1: Percentage of words at different frequency levels,
across sample Cambridge English tests**

(data adapted from Elliott & Wilson, 2013)

Grammar

The language content of listening scripts is also specified in terms of the grammatical structures deemed appropriate at a given level. Clearly, this makes sense in relation to the types of syllabus that test takers will have followed: they cannot be expected to recognise conditionality or the past-before-the-past unless they have been introduced to the forms these concepts take. Fortunately, there appears to be a degree of consensus among curriculum designers about the sequence in which verb tenses or areas such as modality are introduced – a sequence which allows not simply for formal complexity but also for conceptual complexity of the kind that might make demands upon a listener.

On the other hand, in a test of listening to English, some of the most widely used grammatical features – those relating to verb tense and aspect – do not just pose potential challenges in terms of whether and when they have been taught. They also pose challenges (which we tend to overlook) in terms of the low perceptibility of the auxiliary verbs and inflections that mark them. Once again, while test takers may be familiar with a given verb form, much depends upon a) whether they recognise it when they encounter it; and b) how rapidly they manage to map from the form to what it represents conceptually.

Even more rarely considered is the fact (see Chapter 1) that listening has of necessity to take place linearly, with parsing requiring a listener to hold a string of words in the mind until such time as a syntactic pattern can be recognised in them. The cognitive demands that a listening passage imposes upon the listener are thus partly a reflection of how many of those words have to be retained at any one time, whether the order in which they occur follows a standard subject-verb object sequence (Bates & MacWhinney, 1989) and whether they include subordinate as well as main clauses.

An alternative or complementary approach to specifying language content focuses on the kinds of language function that a test taker can be expected to understand. This does indeed bring listening tests closer to the reality of listening beyond the classroom and away from checklist approaches to grammar. However, it is not without its own problems. One of the headaches faced by the 1970s movement towards functional teaching was the question of grading functions by difficulty – since difficulty is a product not simply of conceptual complexity but also of syntactic. It might seem intuitively right to regard 'suggesting' as a pragmatic function which an L2 listener should be capable of interpreting at an early stage; however, the listener needs to distinguish between suggestions that are inclusive (*Let's, Why don't we...?*) or directed at an individual (*Why not ...? Why don't you...?*). What is more, the ways of expressing this function range from syntactically simple (*Let's...*) to syntactically complex (*It might be a good idea to ...*) and from explicit (*You could...*) to less transparent (*Have you ever thought of...?*).

Conclusions for practice

So what conclusions might be drawn for practice?

- It is useful to make a distinction between tests which are targeted at a particular proficiency level as part of an extended suite and those which aim to cover a range of levels. In the case of the former, it is important for test providers to demonstrate that the suite is precisely graded in terms of target language and to provide educators with a set of target linguistic criteria to assist them in preparing potential test takers for the test. The need to demonstrate a rigorous control of grammar and vocabulary is less apparent in the case of tests which range over a number of levels.

- Any approach to controlling the language content of a listening test should ideally be light touch so far as item writers are concerned. One reason is that, perceptually, L2 listening is a highly tentative activity. What a listener *succeeds in recognising* in a recording may have only an indirect relationship to that individual's linguistic knowledge. In addition, we should not lose sight of the extent to which successful listening may be critically dependent upon the use of strategies. Up to about level B2, much listening activity is strategic; and one of the prime requirements is that a learner be capable of inferring the meaning of sections of the recording that have only been partially understood. We can conclude that it is a positive step to include small amounts of language which are beyond the knowledge normally attributed to a learner at a particular level.

- It is not advisable to apply frequency-based vocabulary criteria too rigidly when writing scripts for L2 listening tests. This is partly, again, because inferring a limited number of unknown words from context is a useful strategy for test takers to demonstrate at lower levels of listening. It is also because traditional measures of vocabulary frequency tend to be unreliable either in reflecting the reality of what is taught in the classroom or in representing the range of meanings associated with a particular word as against the frequency of its form. At lower proficiency levels especially, it makes sense to supply item writers with a set of target lexical fields which might override strict frequency criteria. It is also useful to include formulaic phrases alongside single words (Martinez & Schmitt, 2012).

- A figure of of 3500 words has been suggested as a breakthrough target for listening and 6000 as a target for reading. Both figures should be treated with circumspection as they may not take account of differences in the vocabulary demands of different types of text.

- It is not good practice to provide a single frequency-based vocabulary list for stakeholders and item writers which applies to all four skills. At the very least, a distinction should be made between the assumed written vocabulary of a candidate and a smaller assumed oral vocabulary (exceptional cases might be low levels taught communicatively and Young Learners). Up to about level B1+, it should not be taken for granted that receptive oral vocabulary is necessarily the same as productive, given test takers' difficulties in *recognising* known words in connected speech.

- There appears to be a general consensus amongst test providers about the points of grammar that are likely to have been taught at different levels. However, it is again important to bear in mind that, just because a listener has been taught a particular point, it does not necessarily follow that he/she is capable, under pressures of time, of recognising the semantic implications of that feature when it occurs in a particular context.

- It is important not to lose sight of parsing as the means whereby a listener identifies a pattern of grammar in an utterance. Parsing entails holding a string of words in the mind while their grammar is processed; the demands that it imposes upon an L2 listener are determined not only by the frequency and complexity of the grammar point in question but also (given the syllable-by-syllable way in which speech input is processed) the predictability of the sequence of words. In the case of English, this means that standard SVO sequences are easier to process, while passives are problematic in that they present the recipient of the action before the agent.

Length

A second widely employed means of calibrating test difficulty across proficiency levels is by controlling the number of words in the script. A longer text would seem to make greater demands upon attention span and would be likely to require the storage of larger amounts of information. In fact, research evidence on this is unclear as much of it concerns short clips only (Bloomfield et al., 2010: 21–22) and does not sufficiently factor in proficiency.

For lower proficiencies, it certainly makes sense to restrict text length, given the effort which learners have to commit to processing at word recognition level. Item writer guidelines conventionally specify target lengths for scripts which gradually increase through the proficiency levels. However, it is important to be aware that a word count can only be a rule-of-thumb measure. There is no consistent relationship between the words in a script and the running time of the recording. As test material moves up the proficiency scale, the words featured become longer and it becomes more difficult to judge running time solely by counting them.

It is also important to recognise that the question of length is not entirely clear-cut at higher proficiency levels. As already noted, learners at these levels become capable of handling perceptual processes with a high degree of automaticity, thus allowing them to allocate more attention to issues of meaning. An important contributory factor in text difficulty then becomes the amount and complexity of information that a learner needs to handle in order to construct a discourse model. It is not simply the running length of the recording that is an issue but also the density of the information that it contains. A short passage with tightly-packed information can place particularly heavy cognitive demands upon a learner because of the speed at which the information has to be integrated into an overall picture. The contribution of informational density and complexity to text difficulty is discussed further in section 4.6 below; and is investigated in small-scale study reported in Chapter 11 of this book.

While lower proficiency tests often combine short clips of 15 to 30 seconds with longer passages, higher proficiency tests tend to rely mainly or exclusively on the latter. This is partly in recognition of the fact that longer texts impose heavier demands upon the listener's attention. It also seems to reflect a view that (especially in the case of academic listening tests) a longer text is closer to real-world experience – even though, for practical purposes, its duration cannot usually be much longer than (say)

5 minutes. However, the fact is that many breakdowns of understanding do not occur over the course of a complete piece of discourse, but are triggered by problems with local pieces of information. These errors might result in a misrepresentation of just one part of the wider picture or might lead the listener to misconstrue all that comes after them. But the point remains that they originate in relatively small sections of a larger text. A strong case can therefore be made for testing local understanding, even at higher proficiency levels, by means of clips that represent a particular feature of spoken discourse. For example, one might feature a short clip of a speaker outlining what they are about to cover in a talk, on the logic that a failure to make sense of this small section might result in the listener failing to grasp the direction taken by the talk as a whole.

Arguments for varying text length also apply at the lower end of the proficiency spectrum. Testing listening at level A1 is notoriously difficult, and something that test providers tend to fight shy of – partly because of the limited range of language which learners at this level command. One solution is to restrict the input material to very short pieces consisting of only 3 or 4 conversational turns, tested by means of visual multiple-choice options. (Here, the desire of item writers to pepper their material with distractors may need to be resisted). Processing at level A1 is largely driven by the need to identify content words in the input. Short exchanges thus tap much more precisely into the type of processing which learners at this level can employ, and provide clear indications of competence in a way that does not place excessive demands of attention upon the test taker. For similar reasons, recordings at level A2 can be restricted to relatively short exchanges of (say) 7 to 10 turns, if distractors at word level are used. Another expedient, especially favoured by testers in the Far East, is to make use of a 'listen-and-respond' format, in which the test taker is presented with a single utterance and then has to choose the most appropriate of three or four possible responses, usually presented in written form.

In tests which aim to cover a wide band of proficiency levels, reducing the length of texts designed for the very lowest levels not only enables time-efficient assessment; but also brings the additional benefit of preventing higher-level candidates from becoming frustrated at having to handle lengthy tasks that are clearly within their competence. This allows the test provider to include longer texts at higher levels so as to test candidates more rigorously, but to do so without adding unduly to the overall length of the test.

There are, then, many arguments in favour of treating text length more flexibly than at present. However, a major consideration must always be the precise relationship between the text and the number of items that are to be extracted from it. Ideally, keys to items need to be quite widely-spaced to counter-balance the artificial situation associated with most conventional test methods – one where a test taker is provided in advance with pieces of information that have to be stored in the mind and then matched against information in the recording. A useful means of judging the demands being made of the test taker is to divide the length of the recording in seconds by the number of items that have to be answered; this provides an indication of how intensive or well distributed are the responses demanded.

Even so, item density raises quite complex considerations. A combination of a *short recording* and *multiple items* increases the load upon the test taker because of the need to assemble answers under pressure of time. But a combination of a *longer recording* and relatively *few items* also increases the demands upon the test taker since the recording provides many more points of information that offer possible matches for the items and makes it more difficult to determine where the correct answer lies. The general practice seems to be to extend text length rather than item density at higher proficiency levels. The table below shows the ratio across sample tests representing the Cambridge English suite, where KET targets the lowest proficiency level (CEFR A2) and CPE targets the highest (CEFR C2).

Test	Part 1	Part 2	Part 3	Part 4	Part 5	Mean
KET	18.2	11.8	14.4	15.4	18.4	15.64
PET	28.14	24.5	17.5	17.17		21.83
FCE	30.63	19.6	29.43*	29.40*		27.26
CAE	30.5	29.38	37.17	16.4		28.36
CPE	29	28.22	40.8	33.83		32.96

Table 2: Ratio of timings (secs.) to items, across sample tests (Field 2013)

* Figures for Parts 3 and 4 at FCE are reversed to enable comparison with the matching task (Part 4) at CAE level.

Conclusions for practice:

- The length of a listening passage can indeed contribute to its difficulty in that, the longer the passage, the more information a test taker has to carry forward in the mind. But an important variable not to be overlooked is the distribution of the information within the text.
- As vocabulary becomes more complex and multi-syllabic, a listening passage is likely to become longer in duration, even if the number of words is held constant. It may be helpful to specify text length for item writers by means of a word limit accompanied by information on the target speech rate. This enables a rough prediction of the time that a recorded text will take.
- Many breakdowns of understanding take place at a local level, rather than across a piece of discourse as a whole. A strong case can therefore be made for featuring clips in higher proficiency tests as well as in lower proficiency ones, with a view to testing a learner's ability to extract critical information.
- In mixed-level tests, very short texts at A1 level provide valid and reliable indicators of competence in a time-efficient way.
- A useful measure for checking test demands is the relationship between the length of the text in words and the number of items to be answered.

Topic familiarity

It has long been asserted that prior knowledge of a topic considerably assists understanding and reduces the difficulty of a recording (Schmidt-Rinehart, 1994, Jensen & Hansen, 1995). There are a number of reasons why it does so. Topic familiarity enables listeners to anticipate what they will hear; to compensate for points where their decoding of the text is unreliable; to recognise items of vocabulary; and to trace connections between the points that are made. But, while this may be a positive feature in tests which assess the ability to perform in a professional environment, it can cause problems in more general tests of listening, where there is a need to avoid biasing a test in favour of those who have a good prior knowledge of the topic.

Conclusions for practice:

- It is self-evident that, to avoid bias, test setters should use information that is in the public domain and that does not require any specialist knowledge of terminology, concepts or issues. This applies to tests targeting academic listeners across a range of disciplines as well as those designed for general listeners.

- However, we also need to recognise that an essential component of academic and professional listening, whether in L1 or L2, is the ability to draw upon extensive prior knowledge within a certain field. This enables a listener a) to use shared terminology to access meaning; b) to grasp the relevance of new knowledge as it is introduced; c) to provide a conceptual framework into which that new knowledge can be inserted. A case can therefore be made for local-level tests that are specific to a candidate's chosen field. They might be academic (a more reliable means of assessing the ability of entry-level students to deal with lectures in their specialist area); or they might be professional (one example being the domain-specific listening needs of health workers).

Abstractness

It is a challenging task to design listening material at the highest CEFR levels. One solution entails increasing the linguistic and conceptual complexity of the items; but this clearly lacks validity in that the additional difficulty is contributed by reading rather than listening. Another solution adopted by test providers is to specify that recorded material at these levels should be more 'abstract'. Unfortunately, the term is usually poorly defined. There is a danger that abstractness is interpreted in terms of a type of conceptual analysis that even a native listener might have difficulty in following – thus taking the test into cognitive processes beyond those that form a necessary part of listening competence. It is also worth bearing in mind that the most abstract propositions in real-life academic contexts are generally supported by exemplification and explication.

A further device adopted by presentational speakers in order to make abstract propositions more accessible is to express them in metaphorical terms. This feature is also sometimes present in higher-level tests – though there it may well be on the grounds that it ratchets up the perceptual demands of the recording rather than making the discussion easier to follow. One has to question whether this is fair game. Even advanced listeners may sometimes lose track of a line of argument, and fall back on the cues provided by the most salient words. If those words are metaphorical, they may lead to serious and arguably unnecessary misunderstandings. Here is an example (Field, 2013: 123–4) where an abstract topic in a C2 level test is rendered more opaque by the use of imagery:

*As a writer, I find it very exciting that memory and imagination
are part of the same process. When we imagine, we <u>create the
future out of fragments from the past</u>. And when we remember, we
<u>construct pathways</u> in our brains to <u>remake the experience</u> and,
at a certain moment, it's as if <u>the jigsaw comes together</u>, and we'll
accept that as the truth.*

Even a very competent L2 listener approaching this difficult topic is
likely to be seriously misled when the words *fragments, pathways* and
jigsaws are accorded focal stress by the speaker – and likely to end up
further from the point being made rather than closer.

Conclusions for practice:

- The notion that abstractness adds to processing difficulty is intuitively plausible but difficult to interpret in terms of text content and to calibrate across proficiency levels. Abstractness may
  indeed be a useful criterion in tests of reading, where test takers
  have time to reread and reflect upon difficult passages of text.
  However, in texts designed for listening, care should be taken
  not to rely too heavily upon items of abstract vocabulary that
  are difficult to conceptualise or upon lines of argument requiring complex cognitive operations that take us beyond listening
  competence.
- Even advanced listeners may fall back on word-level cues where
  a text is conceptually complex. In these circumstances, the use
  of metaphorical imagery may lead to serious and unintended
  misunderstandings about the topic under discussion.

Discourse type

It is broadly recognised in designing teaching and testing materials that certain types of discourse impose greater processing demands
than others. *Narrative and instructional texts* are widely viewed as
providing suitable material for lower proficiency levels. This is partly
because they can draw upon basic fields of vocabulary and familiar
everyday encounters. But there is also a cognitive rationale for using
them. Texts of this kind generally follow a chronological pattern, so the
discourse-level structure that a test taker has to build is a very simple
one. Candidates are also spared the need to pay heed to connectives,
which are often (like function words) of low perceptibility. An important
exception might be found in the cause-effect relations that sometimes

occur in narration and instruction, but these can often be inferred from world knowledge.

Something similar can be said about *descriptive passages*. They do not follow a chronological structure, but they often require some kind of sequencing of the material – the speaker having to mark a shift from one aspect of the person or object under examination to another. These sub-topics are often quite simple and concrete. A description of a house might begin with the ground floor and progress to the first; a description of a portrait might begin with the face and move on to the clothes; a description of a city might proceed from north to south.

Expository texts are widely used in tests targeting middle proficiency ranges. Their difficulty can be manipulated in relation to the complexity of the information provided and the level of detail. As with descriptive texts, the clarity with which a change of theme is marked may determine how easy it is to follow a speaker. Here, the indications provided may be rather more complex: they might include discourse signals such as *The other thing I wanted to mention…* in conversational exchanges or such as *I now turn to…* in formal presentations. A listener may sometimes be presented with the need to determine whether an incoming point is an extension of the previous one or marks a new direction in the speaker's plan. This kind of decision-making marks an important step towards the building of an overall discourse structure.

There has long been an assumption that *discursive* texts impose the heaviest demands upon listeners. Again, the model of listening outlined in Chapter 1 sheds light on why this should be. Making sense of most discursive material requires quite elaborate discourse construction processes. Listeners have to identify intricate links between points of information that are sometimes conveyed by connectives and sometimes have to be inferred because they have not been expressed explicitly by the speaker. Listeners have to build an argument structure based not simply upon the line of logic that connects the various points but also on the line of logic that shapes the text as a whole. This kind of processing is, as we have seen, rarely in evidence or indeed possible at lower proficiency levels because of the need to focus considerable attention on lower-level recognition processes.

Though texts referred to as 'discursive' are often associated with higher proficiency levels, we should not overlook the fact that there are other types of complex discourse function that could and should be represented, particularly in the context of academic listening. In a study of the demands made by EAP listening materials, Field (2012b) identified several types: *discursive* (for and against), *comparative, persuasive* (single viewpoint), *analytical, critical* and *process-descriptive.*

Conclusions for practice:

- Discourse type provides an approximate means of grading the extent to which a test taker is required to engage in certain types of conceptual processing: e.g. tracing links between pieces of information or building a line of argument across an entire text.
- At lower proficiency levels (say up to level B1), narrative and instructional discourse types provide texts which have an in-built chronological structure that makes them easier to follow. Descriptive texts with clearly marked sub-topics may also be appropriate.
- Expository texts may become more important from Level B1 onwards. In the early stages, they should rely quite heavily upon prominent markers that signal changes of topic and subtopic.
- From level B2 onwards, test takers should be capable of recognising explicit links between points of information. They should be capable of: a) inferring links left unexpressed by a speaker; and b) building a larger argument structure for a text as a whole. This means that discursive texts are increasingly appropriate.
- At C levels, a variety of argument-based texts should be used – extending the notion of 'discussion' to texts that analyse information, that adopt a critical stance to an issue or artefact or that aim to win the listener over to a particular point-of-view. Tasks might include a comparison of the attitudes of two speakers.

Less cited features

Three further features impact upon text difficulty. They occur less frequently in test specifications; but appear to be used informally or intuitively by item writers when calibrating the cognitive demands of texts across different proficiency levels. All three provide additional general indicators of difficulty that can usefully be added to listening test criteria.

Length of utterance

The basic unit of natural speech is an *utterance* –a group of words that begins and ends with a pause. The pause might sometimes represent a hesitation but very often marks a point where the speaker briefly stops speaking in order to plan what to say next (Butterworth, 1980). Utterances often correspond to phrases or complete clauses (Levelt, 1989, Croft, 1995), suggesting that these grammatical units provide the basis for speech planning. Hence the need for listeners to store most or all of an utterance in their minds in order to identify the pattern that holds the words together.

The number of words that a listener can retain varies a great deal. A minor consideration is that the ability to store any information in memory differs somewhat between individuals. A more important one, so far as L2 listeners are concerned, is how much attention has to be given to basic processes such as word recognition and accessing word meanings. As these processes become more automatic, learners become capable of handling longer utterances. The increase in how much can be stored is also supported by the L2 listener beginning to recognise recurrent chunks of language. This lightens the parsing load since incoming utterances can be identified as single items (*shouldadone*) instead of strings of separate words (*I + should + have + done*).

So the length of a speaker's utterances may be an important factor contributing to listening difficulty at lower proficiency levels, where word storage is more limited and more effortful. It makes good sense for test designers to specify the average length in words of the utterances used in recordings at these levels. As learners progress to higher proficiency levels, this measure becomes less of a concern.

Another way of controlling the level of difficulty at utterance level is to introduce (or instruct voice actors to introduce) small increases in the planning pauses between utterances – thus giving the listener more time to assimilate the meaning of what has been heard before proceeding to the next clause. This can be a useful device at the very lowest levels – an alternative to excessively slowing a speaker's speech rate.

Conclusions for practice:
- Utterance length potentially has an impact upon the ease with which a piece of speech can be retained in the mind and parsed. In seems particularly likely to be a factor in listening difficulty for learners at CEFR levels A1 to B1, where parsing and other perceptual operations are effortful. Item writers do well to check the average utterance length of recorded material designed for these levels – or (a rough correlate) the mean length of clauses in scripts.

- It is beneficial to use a format for listening scripts that represents the text as a series of utterances rather than sentences. This not only guides actors' delivery more constructively than punctuation; it also enables item writers to check their scripts so as to ensure that utterances are kept relatively short at lower levels. See examples in Appendix B.
- Slightly extending the length of the planning pauses between utterances gives the listener more time to transition from a group of words to a piece of information.

Information density and complexity

As indicated above, text length provides only a broad indication of the cognitive demands associated with a listening passage. Alongside length, account should ideally be taken of two other indicators: the number of pieces of information included in a recorded text and the complexity of the links between them. These features can be assumed to contribute importantly to the demands that a recording imposes on a test taker. Because listening takes place in real time, with no opportunity for backtracking, a listener has to store up information as it occurs, extrapolating idea units from the words that the speaker uses and then tracing the line of logic that links them. The more information that needs to be processed in sequence and the more complex the connections between it, the greater the demands placed upon the listener.

Conclusions for practice:

- In principle, it is possible to achieve a rough idea of the *information density* of a text by dividing the length of the text in seconds by the number of points of information it contains. In practice, this calculation faces a number of difficulties, not least the need to determine precisely what it is that, for processing purposes, constitutes a unit of information. A later chapter of this book explores whether it is possible to lay down criteria that might assist item writers to calculate the effects of information density.
- Similarly, it might seem easy to gain an idea of the *informational complexity* of a text by identifying the number of between-sentence and within-sentence discourse markers that the text contains and sub-classifying them as co-ordinators or subordinators. Again, (even with the assistance of computer programs) this method is not as clear-cut as it appears. Many logical links between points of information are implicit and not clearly signalled. These have to be inferred by the listener – a task which

is actually *more* cognitively demanding than noting the significance of a marker.

Redundancy, repetition and exemplification

Density of information in a listening passage may be reduced (and the pressure on the listener lightened) by the presence of sections of the text which add nothing new to the task in hand. A speaker might include information irrelevant to the task, repeat points that have been made in order to emphasise them or back up a point by providing a concrete example. This is particularly likely to happen in presentational contexts, where skilled speakers are sensitive to the demands they are placing upon listeners and deliberately pace the introduction of new points of information or reinforce points already made. In principle at least, this allows the listener a brief respite from processing and storing information. Something similar occurs in conversational contexts, where speaker hesitancy and rephrasing allows the listener additional time to make sense of what is being said.

The foregoing comments refer to natural speech. But any or all of the features mentioned can be introduced purposefully into scripted materials in order to thin out their information load. This is particularly useful at the lowest proficiency levels as a means of giving the listener an opportunity to take stock of the information conveyed so far. That said, it is important for item writers not to lose sight of the fact that they may be creating a 'new versus added' conflict. A speaker who repeats a point by paraphrasing it might seem to be assisting the listener. But this may instead result in the listener having to make a decision as to whether the paraphrase represents a repetition or whether the speaker is making a new point.

A conclusion for practice:
Repetition, redundancy and exemplification can reduce the information load of a text. They can serve to spread out a complex argument at higher levels or to slow the flow of information at lower. But care must be taken to not to overlook the possibility that a paraphrase can increase the cognitive load by suggesting that a new proposition is being introduced rather than a repeated one.

5 Recording as speech

One central issue to be addressed in choosing recorded material is whether the input to which candidates are exposed can be said to be representative of a real-world listening event. The concern here is not with 'authenticity' for its own sake, but with the extent to which the nature of the speech sample makes decoding easier or more difficult than it would be in real-world conditions. That said, we should not lose sight of the fact that there are different types of 'normal everyday speech' ranging from informal conversation to more formal transactional dialogue, or from the informal presentational style of a popular broadcaster to the formal monologue of a public lecture.

This leads on to a second major issue. Speech varies enormously – not only according to the nature of the communicative event, but also according to the content being expressed, the speaking style of the speaker, the pitch of the speaker's voice and the speaker-listener relationship. Some of these variables (for example, a rapid speech rate) render the task of listening more demanding, while others (for example, a familiar voice) render it easier. Yet, curiously, test developers tend to spend a great deal of time grading the linguistic features of their scripts but give considerably less attention to the way in which those scripts are delivered. Indeed, it is often the case that the item writer who generated a piece of listening material and its accompanying items never attends the recording session at which his/her ideas are put into the form that the test taker is to encounter.

Origin of recording

The question of representativeness is especially relevant when considering the origin of the recorded material used. In principle, conventional listening tests have a choice of four types of material (Field, 2008a: 272–3):
- *scripted material* recorded in a studio
- *authentic material*, downloaded from available sources such as broadcasts or lectures or recorded in the form of unscripted interviews

- *semi-scripted material* based on transcripts of natural speech (often extensively edited to adapt them to test requirements) and recorded in studio conditions
- *improvised material* recorded in the studio, in which actors are asked to follow certain role-play guidelines.

The big issue with *scripted material* is whether it can be said to constitute a sufficiently representative sample of the speech that test takers might actually encounter in the real world. Texts are heavily dependent upon how sensitive the item writer's ear is to the content and cadences of natural speech. A potential obstacle here is that anyone listening to their first language tends to focus on the content rather than how it is transmitted. We edit out recurrent dysfluencies and hesitations to the point where they are barely noticed; we also edit out our own back channelling and that of interlocutors.

Even more important (and often overlooked) is the nature of the studio recording that is produced. The text is presented to voice actors in the form of a script, which shapes the way in which they deliver their words. It allows them to anticipate what is to come, without the normal planning pauses and hesitations or the need to occasionally re-plan. It employs punctuation but does not mark (for example) where focal stress should fall. One therefore has to question the extent to which the recorded input of many scripted texts can be said to reflect the types of listening demand that real-world speech would make, particularly where informal and interactive delivery is involved.

Clearly, *authentic material* is the ideal. It is becoming increasingly easy to download it from the internet and the sound quality is generally good. Some test developers express concern about pieces of language which fall outside what standard syllabuses prescribe; but the whole point is that this type of content assesses much more validly how well a learner might cope in a real-world situation where one cannot expect the language to be graded. It would be good to see an increasing use of authentic recordings in local testing contexts and in self-study centres. However, so far as the providers of international high-stakes tests are concerned, several problems have historically deterred them from using such material. There are the practicalities – not least, the need to obtain permissions, either from an institution (e.g. in the case of broadcast materials) or from the individuals involved. There is also the fact that much authentic interactional speech may be uninteresting or very loosely structured.

The majority of current listening tests and materials therefore rely heavily upon a mixture of scripted and *semi-scripted* recordings. In the case of the latter, reference is sometimes made to material deriving from 'authentic sources'; but this claim may mean little more than a script that was based upon a newspaper interview. In addition, semi-scripted material is sometimes quite heavily edited, in a way that takes it a long distance from the original source. Reasons for doing this may be to make it conform to syllabus restrictions (for example, eliminating low-frequency vocabulary and idiom). Or they may reflect the item writer's desire to match the text to the demands of the task – notoriously, inserting multiple distractors in order to tailor the content to fit a multiple-choice format.

When all is said and done, transcripts of well-sourced authentic material probably represent the most practical option for many test providers, if the language of the original is largely respected. But, of course, the script that is produced is then handed over to voice actors, with all the issues of delivery that were mentioned above in relation to scripted materials. One way of addressing this is to design new formats for listening scripts which more closely reflect the speech patterns of the original recording. Conventions might be adopted from the way in which discourse analysts transcribe speech in order to distinguish it from written material. Punctuation should be limited to question marks to prevent it impacting on the actor's style. Scripts could give guidance to voice actors on the location of utterance boundaries, on hesitation and planning pauses and on words bearing focal stress. An example appears below.

M: The first time + I realised I'd got a **problem** + was when I went along to a **college** ++ At that time I wanted to be a **plumber** + and they **said** to me + you need to go to **night** school + and they gave me a **pen** + and a **form** to fill in ++ That's when I **realised** + I went **what** does it say? + hey I **can't** + is there anybody that can **help** me? + they said **no** ++ so I said **no** I don't want to **do** this + I said I'm a man who works with his **hands** + I don't need this **night** school

B2 level: semi-scripted.

Finally, there remains the underused option of *improvised recordings*. They, too, are not without their problems. They may require more than one take, adding to studio costs. They may also, on analysis, be found to contain a higher incidence than usual of hesitation pauses – a reflection, not of the nature of informal speech but of the actors rather desperately trying to think of something to say to prolong the dialogue. That said, there is no reason why this kind of material should be limited to interactional dialogues, as it usually is; it surely offers possibilities (particularly in tests of academic listening) for recording impromptu talks.

Conclusions for practice:

- The ideal is to employ authentic material, both conversational and presentational, so far as is possible. However, compromise is understandable, given the difficulties in obtaining this type of material on the scale needed for major international tests. One possibility is to make greater use than at present of in-studio improvisation.
- However experienced voice actors are, they are inevitably influenced by the form of the script which they follow. Test providers need to devise new methods of presenting scripts for studio recording, especially when transcriptions of authentic speech are involved. The aim should be to achieve a delivery that reflects as closely as possible the cadences of natural speech. For further examples of this type of script format, see the sample texts in Appendix B.
- Item writers need to exercise a degree of restraint in editing authentic material for studio recording. Adding distractors indiscriminately increases the information density of a script and runs the risk of rendering it more cognitively demanding than a real-world listening experience.

Visual input

Test providers have so far proved reluctant to embrace recent technological advances that have made video material much more widely available and equipped it with soundtracks of high enough quality for use in assessment. Using audio-only material means that test takers do not have access to important paralinguistic cues based on the speaker's lip movements, facial expressions and gestures, and have no sight of the general context in which an encounter occurs. Such circumstances do indeed arise in certain types of communication (for example radio broadcasts) but they cannot be said to represent the generality of listening events. Test providers need to remain sensitive to the limitations of this type of material and to make appropriate adjustments for the absence of visual cues. In due course, they may need to reconsider their position on video, following neurological evidence (Green, 1998) that information provided by lip-reading is quickly integrated into the listening process.

On the other hand, the research evidence that visual information enhances L2 listening comprehension under test conditions is not as clear as might be assumed. Some studies (Sueyoshi & Hardison, 2005) report clear benefits for video material, while others suggest that video makes no difference (Coniam, 2001) or even that performance declines when either video or still visuals are employed (Suvarov, 2009). One interpretation of the last finding would be that visual information actually serves as a distraction, and that audio material focuses a listener's attention better. Alternatively, it may be that individuals differ in the use they make of the evidence provided by video, with some benefiting and others not.

By contrast, findings on the use of still images to support comprehension are more consistent and accord with Ockey's conclusion (2007: 533) that listeners are not usually helped or motivated by these stimuli. Ginther (2002) cites evidence that test takers benefit from 'content' images which complement the information provided by the recording but not from others that just provide background context. This suggests that pictures of lecturers and students of the kind used in some EAP tests of listening may not add significantly to the test-taking experience. One important aspect of still images that has been little investigated is the role of Powerpoint slides during oral presentations; we are badly in need of more research into how viewing words and images on slides interacts with the speaker's voice. There is some tentative evidence in an eye-tracking study by Suvarov (2015).

Conclusions for practice:
- Long-term, a move towards the use of video materials in listening tests seems likely, particularly where the tests in question are computer-delivered. A strong case can certainly be made in relation to tests of academic listening, where it is now possible to create a split-screen presentation that represents more closely the reality of the lecture context. It might show, for example, PowerPoint slides on one side of the screen and the lecturer (complete with facial expressions and gestures) on the other.

- So long as audio-only tests remain the norm, it is important for test design to incorporate features which compensate for the lack of visual input. A widely employed means of achieving this is to provide a rubric before test takers hear the recording, which gives a clear indication of the topic of the recording and the context in which the listening event occurs. Another is the use of double play.

Monologue vs interaction / presentational vs conversational mode

Most listening tests feature a combination of monologue and dialogue material. This is sound practice as the two formats demand different types of cognitive processing at discourse level. A monologue requires the listener to trace a single line of argument, and one that is likely to be denser and more complex than would occur in a dialogue. By contrast, the logical pattern underlying a conversation has to be extrapolated from the way in which two potentially distinct points of view interact with each other. A listener may be called upon not simply to trace a to-and-fro line of argument but also to compare and contrast the stances taken by the two speakers. Listening to exchanges involving two or more speakers has sometimes been challenged on the grounds that it does not represent a natural interaction since the listener is not involved as a respondent. The fact is, of course, that in real-world contexts L2 speakers may often find themselves part of a conversation of three or more.

Monologue delivery tends to be more closely associated with *presentational* contexts, while dialogue is associated with *conversational* exchanges. These two modes of speech event may vary considerably – particularly in the style of delivery. Broadly speaking, presentational style inclines towards greater precision: a rather slower speech rate, more paced delivery in terms of intonation patterns and more deliberate focal stress. Natural interactional contexts tend to be more casual, with looser speech planning and a less precise articulation, marked by increases in assimilation, elision and reduction. Weak forms of function words predominate – something that (in this author's studio experience) voice actors sometimes fail to deliver consistently. Principled decisions may need to be taken as to the extent to which, in real-world listening encounters, the target test taker will be exposed to either or both types of speech event.

Conclusions for practice:

- It is important to ensure that the speaker's delivery accords with the type of speech event featured (conversational vs presentational).
- Given differences in the processing that takes place at discourse level, a test should ideally include both monologue and interactional material. However, the precise balance between them (and similarly between presentational and conversational material) should reflect the types of listening which the target test taker is likely to have to undertake. A greater proportion of monologue material is clearly desirable in EAP contexts, where the most cognitively demanding encounter takes the form of listening to lectures.

Voice

When hearing any speaker for the first time, a listener has to go through a complex process of adjusting to an unfamiliar voice. L1 listeners are capable of making rapid and highly automatic judgements about the pitch of an individual's voice, the speed at which they speak and the range of their pitch movements (Pisoni, 1997). This is a necessary first step in order to successfully decode what is being said. Indeed, improbable as it may seem, even the ability to recognise the vowels of a language is heavily dependent upon judgements about the fundamental frequency of the speaker's voice (Peterson & Barney, 1952). Some idea of the important role that this process of adjustment (or *normalisation*) plays in all speech events can be gathered from our extraordinary capacity to recognise speakers' voices, even when we have only heard them a few times. Familiarity enables us to tune in rapidly when we meet the same individuals again, without having to repeat the learning process. For the effects of familiarity upon accuracy of processing, see Nygaard & Pisoni (1998).

Normalisation does not come as readily to listeners when the voices in question are using a second language, with its own distinctive pitch ranges and rhythms. There are implications here for test design, especially at lower proficiency levels, where it seems reasonable to allow early-stage listeners a short adjustment period at the beginning of a recording before they have to deal with the first test item. This gives them time to adapt to the voice or voices they hear.

The demands of normalising to unfamiliar voices are obviously greater when the input is in audio form, with no visual information to help differentiate speakers. Two voices in a dialogue do not pose a major challenge to the test taker, especially if the convention is observed of making one male and the other female, so that they are clearly distinguished by pitch. But where there are three or more voices, the demands upon the listener are inevitably stepped up – not simply because of the need to distinguish speakers of the same gender, but also because of the demands of adjusting to several speakers from the outset.

At lower proficiency levels, the issue arises of how great should be the variety of voices across the entire set of recordings in a test. If some of the same speakers recur (especially where there are short clips), familiarity assists the test taker, who does not constantly have to adjust to different voice qualities and styles of delivery. In early-stage tests aimed at Young Learners, it might be desirable to limit the voices to three overall, with clear pitch distinctions – one male, one female, one child. In classroom progress tests, the familiar voice of the teacher might be found preferable to those of strangers.

Conclusions for practice:
- Item writers need to make due allowance for normalisation by ensuring that the early part of a piece of recorded material contains spoken input that is not tested. The normalisation process is also supported if a test permits two plays of the recording – one which enables listeners to become familiar with the speakers' voices and a second to check their understanding of content.
- On the same grounds, it is advisable at lower proficiency levels not to include too many speakers in a single test, especially where there are many short clips. The number of speakers featured makes an important contribution to difficulty because of the demands of adjusting to multiple voices.
- Male/female pairings serve to ensure that voices remain as distinct as possible.

Speech rate

Speech rate is widely recognised as a factor in listening difficulty, though this notion tends to be applied in a rather approximate way in studio recordings. Tests at CEFR levels A1 and A2 generally feature speech which is slower than average conversational speed. Tests at B1 often have a medium-slow delivery speed. Those at level B2 and above commonly feature natural conversational rates.

A principal concern for testers when attempting to provide general specifications for recorded material is how much slower the rate should be at lower levels in order to assist test taker processing (Blau 1990). The author's own measurement of speech rate across a sample test at each of the three lower levels of the Cambridge English suite (Field, 2013) indicated a gradual progression in speech rate. The conclusion was that, that, though slow, the rates at A2 and B1 levels did not fall outside what might conceivably be encountered in real-world contexts (especially where a native speaker is making concessions towards a non-native speaker with limited English). Ramsaran (1978, cited in Gimson 1989:308) puts the lowest level for spontaneous speech in Standard British English at 3.1 syllables per second (equivalent to about 2.1 words per second) and the highest at 5.4 syllables per second (around 3.6 words per second).

The rationale usually given for slowing speech at a lower proficiency levels is that it allows the test taker a better chance to process what is being said. It tends to be assumed that the speed with which the speaker delivers the text is the only factor. In point of fact, early findings by phoneticians (e.g. Goldman-Eisler 1968:24) indicate that what largely distinguishes a 'slow' speaker from a 'fast' one is the amount of pausing that takes place. If a speaker pauses more often, it means that word boundaries are more often marked than they would be in faster connected speech. So voice actors do not need to fall back on a strained or read-aloud style in order to achieve slow speech. Even if the delivery is somewhat slower, they should aim to deliver speech patterns that are as natural as possible and should include contractions and reduced forms. But they should rely principally on regular and slightly longer pauses (0.5 sec) to slow the overall rate down.

At higher proficiency levels, it is important to bear in mind that speech rate is often determined by the nature of the speech event. In this context, a study by Tauroza and Allison (2000) is often quoted, which records the mean speech rates of different types of audio material: radio broadcasts, conversations, interviews and lectures. Some caution has to be exercised about the authors' categories, however, as they were rather loosely represented. Radio broadcasts included read-aloud news alongside monologues and documentary material, on the assumption that all three were scripted. Conversational material was not controlled for familiarity of interlocutors; and the lecture results were for lectures aimed exclusively at NNS audiences. The effects of these variables (both type of material and in speaker style) are seen in the very wide ranges of speech rate in syllables per minute that Tauroza & Allison reported.

That said, the results do provide a useful reminder of the way in which speech rate varies by genre (something testers need to take into account at higher levels). Overall, they illustrate that it is determined by four different factors: the parameters being conversational vs formal and monologue vs dialogue. Commentators such as Calvert (1986: 178) and Griffiths (1992) agree on a mean conversational rate across different speakers of around 200 words per minute or 3.3 words per second. For an authoritative discussion of speech rate, see Laver, 1994: 539–54.

Conclusions for practice:
- If slow speech rates are specified for lower-proficiency tests, it is important that natural intonation contours be maintained by actors so far as possible and that any tendency to read-aloud style be avoided. Once again, this indicates the need for a greater degree of supervision in the recording studio than often occurs.
- A target for test design might be to specify slow conversational speech at Levels A1 and A2 (target: 2.2 to 2.6 wps), medium-slow conversational speech at Level B1 (target: 2.4 to 2.8 wps) and a normal conversational speech rate thereafter (target: 2.8 to 3.4 wps).
- Some tests attempt to challenge C level learners by including speech at quite fast conversational speeds. This needs to be appropriate to the type of material, bearing in mind that tests at these higher levels are more likely to feature monologue presentational material. The natural rate of delivery in such contexts tends to be *slower* than in interactive ones; what most increases the processing demands is the greater complexity of the links between points of information.

Accent

Accent has become somewhat of a cult with certain test providers, who, on no clear evidence, associate achieving a high level of listening competence with the ability to decode speech in a range of varieties of English, including many that may be unfamiliar. This seems to reflect a notion of listening competence as elastic, with skilled listeners capable of stretching their own performance in various directions in order to accommodate to unfamiliar patterns of speech. Canagarajah (2006: 237) invokes a cognitive trait which he loosely terms 'intuition' without making clear to what extent it is, or is not, part of the listening construct. These views of the skill are clearly open to question. For a start, it is obvious that even L1 speakers find difficulty in adjusting to certain distinctive accents among their fellow citizens (see Nygaard & Queen, 2002, cited Nygaard, 2005).

There is no universally accepted theory of how the ability to make sense of speech is acquired, whether in L1 or L2. However, the most convincing account we have suggests that it is an accretional process, with listeners gradually developing points of reference that enable them to identify phonemes, syllables and words. *Exemplar theory* (Nygaard 2008: 405–8, Pisoni, 1997, Goldinger, 1997, Hawkins, 1999: 255–60, Bybee, 2001: 1–18) holds that listeners build up a mental record of spoken word forms based upon multiple traces of voices they have heard. Clopper & Pisoni (2005: 327) adopt a similar view in their review of L1 research into accent and intelligibility, concluding that 'representations [of accents] develop naturally through a person's experience with and exposure to his community and the world at large'.

These versions of events suggest that the ability to decode strongly accented speech is not a matter of adjusting immediately and flexibly to unfamiliar features, but the result of a period of exposure that is often a question of chance. On this analysis, featuring a distinctive L1 regional variety in a listening test runs the risk of bias in that it favours candidates who by happenstance have encountered that particular accent. As has been pointed out quite often (see e.g. Taylor, 2006), the result might well be to favour those who can afford to study English in an English-speaking country as against those who cannot.

The wider arguments in favour of exposing learners to a variety of L1 accents tend to confound two very different issues. One (particularly sensitive in Britain, where accent has social as well as regional associations) is the unacceptability of viewing one variety as 'correct' or 'prestige' and dismissing others as of lower standing. Here, reference is sometimes made to the notion of Received Pronunciation (RP), though it is a term long distrusted by phoneticians[1]. The other issue is the entirely

---

[1] Partly on the grounds that nobody could agree on precisely what it referred to (anything between the idiolect of Prince Charles and the variety spoken in the larger part of southern Britain). Roach (2000:3) describes the term *RP* as 'old fashioned and misleading'.

distinct question of choosing an accessible and widely dispersed variety of English which can be used as a model for second language pronunciation teaching and by extension for the early stages of second language listening. The first issue is a value-laden one; the second is purely a practical one.

When discussing the role of accents in testing, it is important not to lose sight of the heavy demands that any L2 test of listening already places upon candidates. They have to normalise to a variety of unfamiliar voices that vary not only in pitch but also in speech rate and precision of articulation (see the previous two sections in this chapter). In a test that contains a number of dialogues, a listener may encounter a large number of such voices, and has to accommodate to each of them in order to perform even basic operations like distinguishing vowels. By adding into this mixture a variety of accents, the test designer considerably heightens the demands of an already-difficult task. This is especially true when, as sometimes happens, a single dialogue features speakers of two different varieties, and the unfortunate listener has to switch between the two.

The test takers most affected are those at lower proficiency levels who, as noted earlier, have to dedicate much of their attention to decoding speech at phoneme level and to recognising known words. Introducing accent as an additional variable at these levels inevitably reinforces their tendency to focus upon bottom-up perceptual cues, and diverts them even further from large-scale issues of meaning. A sensitive approach would ensure that, at these levels, test takers only have to cope with one or two standard varieties.

A further consideration is that, while English does indeed possess an interesting range of social and regional accents, they are not easy to pick up. The reason is that the most important differences between the L1 varieties of English lie in their vowels and diphthongs (Wells, 1982). Full vowels provide reliable phonetic cues for listeners (even L1 listeners) because they are much longer in duration than consonants. Stressed syllables containing those vowels thus play an important part in identifying words (Grosjean & Gee, 1985). This means that encountering an unfamiliar accent of English is likely to have a disproportionate effect upon word recognition, as compared with languages such as Spanish, where variation lies mainly in the consonants. Those designing tests of English should thus never underestimate the impact of accent upon comprehension.

Then there is the question of which varieties to choose. It is obviously reasonable, in an age of mass communication, to assume some exposure to international L1 varieties of English (US, British, Australian/NZ) among middle to high proficiency test takers. However, commentators have also raised the question of whether the choice of accents should include the varieties spoken by the huge worldwide population of non-native speakers of English. Isn't a language learner more likely to encounter one of these (the argument goes) than an L1 speaker?

The first obstacle here (one curiously little mentioned) is the need to determine exactly what constitutes an L2 variety. The easy assumption is that it is a version of English with traces of L2 phonological features. But the briefest pause for reflection will raise concerns about this notion. Surely the variety spoken by any individual depends heavily upon their level of proficiency? Surely it depends upon the variety of English (American, Australian, British) that they have been taught? And whether they have lived in an English-speaking community? And what contexts they have used their English in? With this in mind, the idea that a recording in a test can feature a 'representative' version of an L2 variety seems rather illusory. And that is without considering the possible impact of regional L1 varieties (think European vs Brazilian Portuguese, Swiss-German vs Berliner, Castellano vs Gallego, Milanese vs Napolitano) and regional languages (think Cantonese vs Mandarin) on the way their speakers handle the pronunciation of English.

A second major flaw in this idea is that its proponents tend to overlook the fact that intelligibility is not simply a property of the speaker, but the result of a trade-off between speaker and listener. Amongst those likely to be using English as a medium of communication, there are literally thousands of possible combinations of speaker L1 and listener L1. So which should feature in any major international test directed at a wide range of listener L1s? A major issue here is, again, the possibility of test bias (Major et al, 2002: 24, Geranpayeh & Taylor, 2008: 4). In any international test of listening, we cannot rule out the likelihood of test takers being presented with a recording of speakers of their own L2 variety. The more common the L2 variety, the greater this likelihood: consider the implications, for example, of including Mandarin-accented speech in a test. There is also the likelihood that an L2 variety from a country adjacent to the test takers' own will be easier for them to process than it would for candidates on the other side of the world.

These issues were addressed in a comprehensive study by Harding (2011), using L2 speakers of English rated as 'highly intelligible'. Harding's results were mixed: he found strong effects of familiarity in relation to one of his nationality groups and one of his two recordings, but they were not consistent across all his participants. Nevertheless, they echo results obtained by others (e.g. Major et al., 2002) and are sufficient to raise concerns about the dangers of bias if L2 accents are used in international tests of listening. Harding goes on to consider the viability of what he terms a weak ELF ('English as a Lingua Franca') approach to the question; but even here he recognises a major stumbling block in the need to reach agreement across a range of listeners and L1s on the perceived level of intelligibility of the speakers used in a test[2].

So far as local and regional testing is concerned, it may indeed be possible to determine precisely the L2 varieties which a learner is most likely to encounter, and to target the recorded material accordingly. However, any international high-stakes test of listening runs the risk of assessing candidates on their understanding of English accents that they may never have encountered and may never need to encounter. For thoughtful reviews of the *lingua franca* arguments in testing, see Taylor, 2006 and 2009.

Conclusions for practice:
- The ability to competently decode speech in a regional variety of English should not be conceived as a kind of tolerance for phonological divergence that is part of general listening competence. It is likely to be serendipitous, and based upon chance encounters with speakers of the variety, which some test takers may have had and others not.
- Testers thus do well to adopt a cautious approach to accents in L2 listening tests. It makes sense to feature a single accent of English at the lowest proficiency levels: This could be the one that features most prominently in local listening materials or it could be the local variety in certain contexts (e.g. parts of Africa using English as a medium of communication). At (say) B1 level, the range could be extended to two international varieties:

[2] Jenkins's (2000) *Lingua Franca Core* does not provide a solution here, though it is sometimes cited as listing those features of L2 English speech that ensure maximum intelligibility worldwide. It seems highly unlikely that this kind of generalisation could ever be achieved, given the multitude of possible speaker-listener L1 pairings. The original set of features was in any case based upon a very small sample of speaker-listener pairs whose first languages were not controlled for.

perhaps General American and Standard British.[3] These terms are intentionally chosen because both embrace the possibility of including certain regional variations which would be intelligible to most or all native speakers. It is likely that test takers will have had exposure via the internet to these or similar forms.

- At B2 level, listeners have begun to acquire decoding processes which more closely resemble those of a native listener, thus allowing them more working memory capacity to deal with apparent inconsistencies in the signal. This provides favourable conditions for a progression towards the inclusion of a range of standard international varieties of English (including Australian/ NZ and South African).

- Regional varieties of English representing relatively small popu-lations should be avoided if the only reason for their inclusion is to challenge the test taker. This is no reflection upon the standing of such varieties; it is simply a matter of fairness to the test taker, who may or may not have been exposed to them.

- The inclusion of non-native varieties would also seem to be very problematic in international and high-stakes tests because there are too many speaker-listener combinations for the test designer to avoid potentially favouring test takers who come from the same region as the speakers and disfavouring others who do not. At higher proficiency levels, an exception might be found in the varieties used in countries where English serves widely as a lan-guage of national communication.

- Featuring two different varieties within a single dialogue imposes unfair processing demands on low to mid-proficiency test takers.

The role of the recording

Let us summarise a few of the more general points raised in this chapter and the last.

It is important not to lose sight of the fact that it is the recorded material, not the script, which forms the input on which the test taker is assessed. An item may target very precisely what the writer has identified as a salient point in the script; but it is not impossible that the point will be

---

[3] *General American* refers to a broadly comprehensible type of North American English which does not have strong regional characteristics. The term *Standard British* was a term proposed by Gimson (1989) in order to move away from the poorly defined notion of RP and implications of prestige.

downgraded in prominence by the speaker, making it harder for the test taker to detect and thus increasing the difficulty of the task. Items thus need to be checked quite closely against recorded content, with account taken of the perceptual salience of the keys within the recording and any confusing signals provided by phenomena such as speaker back-channelling. In determining which points of information in a recorded text are to be the focus for items, it is important to take account not only of their lexical and syntactic complexity but also their prominence relative to other points. This information cannot be derived if decisions about items are based solely upon a tapescript.

A second consideration is the extent to which a piece of recorded material used in a test can be said to represent the type of input to which a test taker would be exposed in a real-life context – and thus to generate processes which are generally representative of those that the test taker would employ in the world beyond the test. The ideal is clearly to use authentic material; but if this proves difficult and a test provider relies instead on re-recording authentic texts, then the way in which the script is presented to studio actors plays an extremely important part in deciding how natural the delivery is and how closely it resembles everyday speech.

It should also be recognised that, alongside linguistic and informational content, phonological and phonetic aspects of the speaker's delivery play a major part in determining the difficulty of a particular recording. In practice, features such as speech rate or precision of articulation are often not controlled – partly because of a division of labour between the item writer, the test designer and the studio technician. It is good practice to specify the type of speaker delivery when designing listening test guidelines, with due account taken of the proficiency level being targeted. Instructions can then be added to tapescripts by item writers in order to guide the recording process.

Finally, a further area of concern can be found in the recording-as-text. Alongside traditional linguistic criteria relating to syntactic difficulty and lexical frequency, it is important to take account of textual features which may contribute to processing difficulty. They include length of utterance (the longer the utterance, the more the test taker has to hold in mind while parsing) and density and complexity of information. Drawing on evidence of how listening skills develop over time, it has been suggested that the former may be more of an issue for lower proficiency test takers and the latter more challenging for higher-level ones.

TASK CHARACTERISTICS

6 Listening test conventions

Over the years, a number of conventions have grown up concerning the way in which the recorded material and test items are delivered to the test taker.

Modality

Test items are generally presented in written form. One reason is that there tend to be a large number of them, so that a permanent record of what is being asked (one that does not have the transitory and time-constrained nature of the listening signal) is necessary to assist the listener. Another reason is that, above the lowest proficiency levels, items can be quite complicated and to ask questions orally might impose an unreasonable burden upon the listener's memory.

However, presenting items in this way runs the risk of loading at least some of the processing elicited by the test on to reading[1]. This is particularly the case when, at higher proficiency levels, the concepts that are targeted become more complex. At lower levels, one way of minimising the reading load is to make use of summaries or simulated forms, in which the test taker has to insert missing words. Another is to make use of graphic formats, such as maps or plans of buildings, which test takers have to label.

Clearly, the use of written items addresses the needs of major international high-stakes tests – particularly in relation to ease of delivery when a large number of test takers is assembled at a test centre. It also tends to be accepted unquestioningly in the case of local tests; but there is no reason why this should be so. In classroom testing that makes use of short clips, the test administrator might instead ask an oral question after each clip. With longer listening passages, the test administrator might pause the recording after (say) a third of it has been played and ask two or three oral questions about what has been understood so far. It is even possible

[1] A rather disturbing finding by Milton, Wade & Hopkins (2010) was that both phonological and orthographic vocabulary were contributory factors in candidates obtaining a mid-level score or higher in an IELTS test (though admittedly the latter effect was less powerful).

to edit a piece of recorded material, embedding spoken questions into it after each minute or so of listening followed by a pause that gives learners time to write answers.

Pre-presentation

Because there is usually a set of up to 10 questions, test takers need time to read them. The questions are therefore conventionally presented before the recording is heard, with 40 seconds to a minute allowed for reading. There are good reasons for pre-presentation. If questions are not presented until after the candidate has heard the recording, it means that the listening that takes place may lack direction and focus. In addition, there are likely to be strong memory effects, with test takers with superior memory capacity able to retain much more of the passage in order to answer the questions.

However, the pre-play tradition is not without its problems. It primes test takers to predict what they are going to encounter in the recording (even to the point of making guesses as to which MCQ option is the most likely or to constructing a schema on the strength of items designed for gap-filling). This may influence and even distort what they think they hear. It also creates a *divided attention* situation (Wickens, 1984, Paschler & Johnson, 1998), with the listener having to carry forward written items in the mind and to crosscheck their recall against the written original at the same time as listening. But perhaps the most damaging effect is in the encouragement of test-wise strategies by candidates, who try to map from key words in the written items to spoken words in the text. There is evidence (see e.g. Field, 2012a) that this type of strategic behaviour leads to a greater degree of processing at word rather than clause level and prevents test takers from building up a wider discourse representation.

Double play

In many international tests, the test taker is allowed to hear the recording twice. The principal argument in favour of this practice is that it compensates test takers for the fact that an audio presentation does not allow them the opportunity of seeing paralinguistic signals such as facial expression, gesture or lip movement or indeed the physical context in which the talk or conversation took place. There are also arguments related to (for example) the need for listeners to normalise to one or more unfamiliar voices in the recording.

However, the convention has recently been challenged on the grounds that, in a real-world situation, a listener is unable to hear a piece of spoken input more than once. The assertion is in fact not entirely true these days, given the playback facilities that exist for radio and TV programmes, university lectures, etc. Clearly, too, if one is engaging in interactive listening, there is always the possibility of asking the speaker for clarification. Despite this, opponents continue to claim that the double-play convention unnaturally reduces the difficulty of a test; and opinion remains divided as to its costs and benefits. On these grounds, some major tests (particularly tests of academic listening such as TOEFL and IELTS) restrict candidates to a single play.

A recent British Council funded research study (Field 2015) investigated the impact of double play upon scores and score bands and upon the cognitive behaviour of test takers. The conclusions were that:

- Double play does raise scores but by a relatively small amount (see also the large-scale study by Ruhm et al. 2016) and one that varies between test takers.
- Double play does not seem to bias test scores in favour of test takers at either lower or higher proficiency levels. It does not diminish the differentials between score bands; if anything, it marks them out more sharply.
- Double play appears to result in individual scores for lecture-listening that are more closely aligned with the scores obtained in other types of listening task.
- The majority of test takers reported themselves as listening in a focused way during the first play with a view to locating information critical to the questions; then listening more generally to the recording as a piece of discourse during the second play. Generally, they claimed to achieve a better and broader understanding of the content of the recording as a result of hearing it twice.

It would appear that playing a recording twice does not interfere with final score differentials. It does indeed compensate for a lack of visual evidence. But, more importantly, it also compensates for the highly artificial nature of the types of task that are set in tests of listening. A majority of test takers affirmed that they used the first play in order to orient themselves to the listening passage and to get a general impression of where information was located (as they might in scanning a reading text); they then used the second play to confirm the answers to questions. In other words, on at least one play, they were engaging in a type of listening that could be said to approximate more closely to that of the real world than what usually occurs when an individual has a one-off chance to find answers to questions. Several participants reported that the opportunity of hearing the recording twice had the effect of reducing the *listening anxiety* (Bekleyen, 2009) which is a by-product of the transitory nature of the signal.

A more adventurous solution to the issue of whether to permit a double play or not is to leave it up to the individual test taker. This is obviously only possible in computer-delivered tests, where the timing of the listening session can be flexible; it was adopted, for example, in the original version of the British Council's Aptis test. The logic is that a weaker listener might take the opportunity to listen to a recording two or more times, whereas a stronger one would be capable of extracting answers on a single hearing and would get on faster with the test. However, in order to ensure that the final score reflects this difference of proficiency (and/or that some adjustment is made for the advantage accorded to the less able candidate), it arguably makes sense when using this format to add some means of measuring the time taken by each candidate and to factor it in to the scoring. It would, of course, have to be made plain to candidates that timing was a consideration in assessing their performance; and it might not work very reliably if very low level listeners simply fell back upon guesswork in order to log a faster time.

But the biggest concern about this free-choice approach is that it takes no account of the different personalities of those who take the test. Far from reducing the pressure upon a test taker lacking confidence, it seems likely to increase it. The effort of decision making (*Should I rewind or do I have more than a 60% level of confidence in my provisional answer?*) must certainly add to, rather than detract from, whatever listening anxiety the individual is experiencing.

Order of presentation

It is clearly problematic to expect test takers to carry forward up to (say) eight propositions in their minds when they are undertaking a gap filling task, and up to 32 when they are undertaking a four-option multiple choice task. Two conventions have therefore developed to assist the mapping from written item to key in the recording. The first is to present test items in the same order as the information occurs in the recording (Buck, 2001: 138). The second is to space items out relatively evenly, allowing the test taker time to internalise each response before proceeding to the next (Brindley, 1998). These conventions are not without some cost, however. They unfortunately encourage further test-wise strategies, with test takers assuming after a certain delay that they have missed the answer to question 1 and choosing to move on to question 2 (Field 2012a). They also encourage test takers to construct a set of sequenced expectations about what they will hear before they have even been exposed to the recording.

Rubric

Where audio recordings are in use, item writers are usually expected to provide some minimal information about what the listener is going to hear in order to compensate for the lack of visual input. A good rubric of this kind should ideally cover three important points of information: how many speakers there are; the domain in which the speech event happens; and the topic. The rationale is that listeners usually come to an encounter with expectations in mind that are shaped by these pieces of knowledge. An additional component of the rubric might specify the goals of the listener in order to provide a general purpose for listening:

Look at the plan of an apartment. A woman is moving her furniture into the apartment. She is telling a man where to put it.

You will hear four people (A, B, C and D) talking about sport in schools. What is the attitude of each one?

You will hear a radio programme where two computer specialists, a woman and a man, are interviewed about the internet. Listen for the positive and negative points that they make.

Computer-based solutions

Increasingly, national and international tests of listening are available in computer delivered as well as paper-based formats. The advantages of Computer Based Testing (CBT) to test providers are many: flexibility in the timing of tests, the possibility of reaching a much wider population, reduced costs. There are advantages to the test taker, too – including a reduction in the anxiety associated with mass testing in a centre and even the possibility of allowing individuals to exercise greater control over the material that reaches them (choosing whether or not to re-listen to parts or all of a recording was an example cited earlier).

Perhaps the greatest advantage of CBT – one that has been insufficiently recognised – is that it enables test designers to deal effectively with some of the problematic aspects of the test conventions discussed in the preceding sections. Most critically, whereas test items on paper have, for logistical reasons, to be distributed before the test takes place, computer delivery can exercise control over the moment at which items are presented. This enables a test designer to sidestep the old problem of providing candidates with too much advance information before they listen. Presentation of the questions (with adequate time to read them) can take place after a first play of the recording; and the questions can then be answered during or after the second play (Field 2013, 2015). Sherman (1997) reported that presentation of questions between plays assisted performance to a greater degree than when it occurred pre-play.

An alternative is to adopt a format where a recording is heard in its entirety during a first play. When it is played for a second time, it is then divided into three sections, with a pause between each. Up to three MCQ questions can be presented on-screen before each third of the text is heard again, thus ensuring purposeful listening without encumbering the test taker with a whole battery of questions.

In terms of cognitive validity, an approach of this kind represents a major advance over the traditional pre-presentation of questions. It eliminates the use of test-wise strategies in which candidates create expectations about what they will hear on the basis of items that they have seen in writing. It also reduces the construct-irrelevant demands of committing a number of test items to memory in advance of listening. This enables test takers to listen, on a first pass, in a way that resembles much more closely the type of listening that takes place in real-life, without the unnatural pressures of having to locate answers to specific questions. It encourages candidates to process the content of the recording in a way that takes account of wider issues at discourse level rather than simply local facts. In addition, the approach provides the listener with the opportunity of normalising to the voices in the recording before listening more carefully on a second play to check understanding.

7 Task formats

Conventional formats

A number of standard formats are used in tests of L2 listening. They include: multiple-choice, visual multiple-choice, gap filling, form filling, multiple matching, labelling and (at young learner levels), drawing lines to link graphics. These particular types are favoured because they conduce to easy marking. Another consideration is that most or all of them are likely to be familiar to test takers before they come to take one of the standard international tests. However, test designers should not lose sight of the fact that the operations demanded of learners by any of the formats cited are highly specific to the testing context and indeed may demand cognitive processes that are considerably more demanding than those that would apply in a real-world listening context. The conventional formats used in listening also implicate other skills. *Selected response* formats such as MCQ may make demands (sometimes heavy) on a test taker's reading proficiency, while *constructed response* formats like gap-filling require raters to distinguish criteria relating to comprehension from others which reflect competence in reading or writing.

Many national tests of listening and even some international ones rely solely or mainly upon a three-option or four-option multiple-choice format. However, using MCQ as the only format flies in the face of a prevailing assumption that one needs to cover a variety of methods in a test because of the way in which test method impacts upon candidate behaviour (Brindley & Slatyer, 2002). Using a mixture of formats brings the following advantages:
- Most formats provide prior information about the recording, but they do so in different ways. Varying them means that test takers cannot fall back on a routine set of test-wise strategies.
- Test formats sometimes draw upon cognitive skills (e.g. decision-making or holding multiple options in one's mind) that are nothing to do with listening. Test takers vary markedly in the extent to which they possess these skills. A test with a single format might thus be biased against test takers with particular mental sets. A test with multiple formats reduces this possibility.

- It may be desirable to adjust the format chosen to fit the proficiency level being targeted. This might address the issue of limited L2 literacy at lower levels, and consequent difficulties in reading written items.

From a cognitive perspective, a further consideration is the importance of choosing formats which allow the item writer to elicit a range of different listening processes. Certain formats including MCQ and multiple matching enable an item writer to range quite freely across the levels of processing which contribute to listening (see Chapter 1). These formats can focus equally on local factual information, main point, inference, speaker attitude, links at discourse level and argument structure. Advantage of this flexibility should especially be taken at higher levels, where the full range of listening processes is rarely adequately represented in current test design, and item writers continue to exhibit a heavy preference for focusing upon discrete local points. By contrast, the gap-filling format (for all its resemblance to note-taking) promotes a focus at word level and encourages item writers to target local information, thus limiting the range of processes covered.

There follow some brief comments on several commonly used formats.

- **Multiple-choice**. The MCQ format has some important advantages in terms of ease of computer marking and familiarity. However, one should not overlook its well-documented limitations (Freedle & Kostin, 1999, In'nami & Koizumi, 2009, Wu, 1998). They include a heavy reliance upon reading items that may be quite complex and finely discriminated; and the provision of written information about the recording (some of it potentially misleading) in advance of listening.

  Often overlooked, but perhaps of greatest concern, is the fact that the MCQ format requires the test taker to perform an operation that is considerably more cognitively demanding than what would happen in real-life listening. We tend to assume that the sole goal of the test taker is to identify the correct option out of three or four; but this is not how human beings operate. Test takers feel themselves obliged not simply to seek a match for the correct option but also to disqualify the incorrect ones.

- **Visual multiple-choice**. Providing visual MCQ options is a sound way of ensuring that lower proficiency learners do not suffer from the effects of their limited reading skills. It avoids the conflict of using written items in a test of oral skills and of dividing test takers' attention between two types of information. It is worth noting that visual MCQ listening tasks can take a number of different forms.

- Test taker hears a single sentence or a short clip and identifies the correct visual of three or four.
- Test taker hears four sentences distinguished by letters (A,B,C,D) and writes the appropriate letter against each visual.
- Test taker identifies the order in which visuals are mentioned and numbers them from 1 to 4.
- Test taker has to connect a list of options to the correct places on a map or plan.

Care has to be taken to ensure (particularly in the first of these task types) that the distinctions between visuals are not so fine that they challenge the visuo-spatial awareness of the test taker; this may be an issue when testing young learners. There may also be cultural problems in using maps in certain parts of the world.

■ **Oral multiple-choice**. The possibility of using oral multiple-choice items is widely rejected by listening testers, for the very obvious reason that it is unreasonable to expect test takers to carry forward in their minds complex choices that have been presented auditorily. However, this format can still prove useful at lower proficiency levels, where it counters the problem of limited L2 reading skills and increases the validity of a test. The only proviso is that certain basic criteria need to be observed. The options given (ideally three) have to be concrete, sharply distinct from each other and (most important) limited to one or two words. Ideally, a single question should be used in conjunction with a short clip of around 30 seconds and might be presented both before and after the clip. Test takers simply need to write the letter of the correct option.

Oral MCQs can even be used at higher levels in a way that taps very closely into the process of building a simple discourse representation. Here, the items are presented during pauses inserted in a longer recording – perhaps a maximum of three, each requiring the test taker to sum up what has been heard in the preceding section.

■ **Gap filling**. Gap filling might appear to be a sound way of reporting on what has been heard in that it resembles the real-world process of note-taking. However, we cannot overlook the fact that it engages both reading and writing alongside the target skill – with item writers having to devise lists of acceptable responses so that test takers are not penalised for wrong spelling. Those who employ this task also tend to underestimate the demands that it imposes upon the test taker, who has to coordinate reading, writing and listening and to do so under pressures of time. This is not only a complex metacognitive operation; it also runs the risk of divided attention effects (Paschler & Johnson, 1998), with the test taker having to understand and produce written texts at the same time as listening. A study of experiences during an IELTS listening test (Field, 2012a) provides testimony to the challenges faced by the test taker.

A further problem associated with gap filling is the fact that the frames to be filled supply test takers with, in effect, a summary of the content of the recording. This provides them with advanced knowledge of what they will hear and encourages them to construct a schema for the listening passage in advance of hearing it. Despite this, the method itself seems to promote processing by test takers at the level of the word – understandably, because it is word-level information that they have to provide in their answers. As Field (2013: 131) concludes after analysing the content of sample tests: 'The sentence frame may well paraphrase information from the text, but the words to be inserted are often to be taken verbatim from the recording and rarely from a larger unit than a lexical chunk'. See Buck (2001: 82) for a similar comment.

■ **Multiple matching**. A great advantage of this format over the others discussed is that items for multiple matching do not need to follow the order of their mention in the recording. The format can also greatly reduce the amount and complexity of the written material that the listener has to process and thus avoid the close reading necessary with many MCQ items.

It does not, like gap-filling, provide the listener with an advanced knowledge of the argument structure of the recording to be heard. However, instead, the listener has to hold a series of propositions in the mind which can occur in any part of the recording, or even not occur at all, and to match them against supporting evidence. It is therefore important that test designers do not lose sight of the fact that multiple matching runs the danger of drawing upon competencies which fall beyond the listening construct and which relate to the test taker's ability to manipulate information. The best way of dealing with this potential problem is to limit the number and complexity of the options to be matched to a maximum of (say) eight. It is also advisable to permit a second play of the recording when using this particular format.

- **True/false.** There is a long history of scepticism concerning the reliability of this format, given the 50% likelihood of a correct response. One solution has been to extend the choices open to the test taker by adding a category of *Not mentioned*. However, particularly with expository texts, it can sometimes prove difficult for an item writer to make a clear distinction between an item which is not correct and one which is not mentioned. An adaptation of the format which performs well with simple discursive conversations (e.g. whether to go by train or car) is one where the test taker has to decide whether a view was expressed or not and by which speaker.

Conclusions for practice:
- Most standard formats run the risk of favouring test takers with particular cognitive bents. To avoid possible bias, it is strongly advisable to use two or more formats in a test of L2 listening.
- Item writers must be sensitive to the part played by other skills (particularly reading) in standard test formats. With this in mind, they need to limit the syntactic and propositional complexity of written items, and particularly of MCQ options. At higher levels, it is particularly important that they resist the temptation to load difficulty on to the items rather than the recording.
- Non-written varieties of the MCQ format are worth consideration, particularly for testing at lower proficiency levels
- While the gap filling format may appear to be superficially representative of a real-life listening activity, item writers need to be aware of the heavy cognitive demands that it imposes upon a test taker and of the possible divided attention effects associated with it.
- It is important to think of the standard formats in terms of the listening processes they elicit. MCQ and multiple matching are capable of representing a wide range of processes, while (contrary to what might be expected) gap filling tends to encourage a focus on word level processing.

- Most conventional formats possess the disadvantage that they provide the test taker with advance information of the recording that would not be available in a real-world listening context. Multiple matching tasks carry the advantage that they do not need to follow the order of mention of points within a recording.

Some thoughts on scoring

Although the standard test formats just discussed sometimes require cognitive and/or language skills which go well beyond what real-world listening demands of the listener, their advantages are that they are easy to deliver and easy to mark. What is more, they are generally familiar to learners within their educational context. The majority of them are described as 'objective' – meaning that the scores are not based upon the judgements of an experienced assessor but derived by totalling the number of correct responses given by a candidate. The implication is sometimes drawn that this makes them more reliable than impressions based upon the kind of rating scales employed in tests of writing and speaking.

However, this impression is open to challenge. The final score is not as clear-cut as the score at the end of a football match; it is closely dependent upon informed but nevertheless subjective choices by the item writer in determining which points of information to target and what questions to ask about them. A guiding consideration may be to choose those keys in the text that appear to contribute importantly to the passage as a whole and (especially in the case of lower proficiency tests) are clearly expressed by the speaker. But compromises sometimes have to be made. It may be that the item writer can only identify seven major points of information out of the ten that are needed; in that case, the remaining questions have to focus on more peripheral pieces of information that a competent listener might skip in other circumstances. Furthermore, as already noted, the item writer may not even get to hear the recording to check that the information targeted is perceptually salient, but might base the questions on a written script at an early stage of the test production process.

There is also the matter of how comparable are the cognitive processes that are elicited by the items. Item writers are prone to talk about 'getting the feel' of a listening passage (Salisbury, 2005). In one version of a test, they might focus mainly upon factual information; in another version of the same test, they might rely to a much greater degree on asking learners to infer information or to identify speaker attitudes. Finally, there is the question of the wording of the items: how easy or difficult is it for the text taker to map from these sources (usually written) to the recording? Do the items include key words that also occur in the recording, or paraphrases? Does an item include two or three distinct propositions in it that have to be checked against the recording?

These issues are obviously addressed with some care by major international test providers, who take care when approving newly written versions and trial them intensively before they go live. But the fact is that there is a limit to what even the most finely-tuned statistical analysis can tell us. There are simply too many variables in a typical test for us to say with entire confidence 'this low-scoring item entails demanding listening' and 'this high-scoring item is easy'. While some variables do indeed reflect the nature of the listening construct, others may be by-products of the method used, the questions asked and the relative importance and perceptual prominence of the information targeted. Statistical analysis may sometimes show up an item as too demanding for the level for which it has been designed; but it may simply be that a subset of test takers at that level have not fully mastered one of the basic processes that one might normally expect at that level (e.g. identifying the main point or reporting the speaker's goals).

The solution in terms of local testing is to think outside the box and avoid conventional formats. If test taker numbers are relatively small, less importance attaches to ease of delivery and ease of marking. Freer formats can be adopted that require a degree of subjectivity on the part of the marker. They might include: note-taking, summary completion, oral reporting, form-filling, labelling visuals and marking directions on maps, putting statements in order or organising them under headings.

In certain relatively rare circumstances, a tester might need to provide concrete evidence that illustrates the listening skills of an individual or a group. Two examples in the author's own experience have been: demonstrating the L2 listening proficiency of an individual questioned by the police and assessing the extent to which a cohort of young learners is competent to move on to English Medium Instruction (EMI). Here, a simple score will not suffice; the authorities in question require evidence to support any decision. Evidence of this kind is easy to obtain in the case of the productive skills: speaking can be recorded and writing gives rise to a script. But it is by no means easy when the skill to be assessed is listening.

The solution arrived at in the second project that was mentioned (Field, 2014b) employed three basic tasks. In the first, individual learners were interviewed singly and asked a series of questions. These began with questions that were short in duration, simple in syntactic structure and easily predictable or inferable from key words (*What class are you in?*). They then gradually increased in length and difficulty (e.g. to *What work do you want to do when you're older?*). A second task was based upon the type of elicited imitation exercise sometimes used by researchers to test implicit knowledge of grammar (Erlam, 2006). In this, the researcher speaks a series of sentences exemplifying certain syntactic patterns and asks the learner to repeat as accurately as possible what was heard. Again, the initial statements to be repeated were simple in vocabulary and syntax and referred to familiar domains; they gradually increased in length and complexity. Items ranged from *I like reading* to *I showed my friends a photograph.* In the third task, the researcher spoke a series of incomplete sentences and asked the learner to compete them (*She's drinking...,* *Could you please open...*) Performance on the tasks was recorded, and provided evidence as to the point at which each individual's listening proficiency became inadequate.

It became apparent in the EMI study (Field, 2014b) that a small team of four listening specialists could attribute CEFR levels to the various speakers with a very high degree of reliability (either 75% or 100% agreement). Here, then, is a method of demonstrating listening proficiency that is externally verifiable. It is, of course, time-consuming, but certainly offers an interesting possibility for progress tests in classroom contexts.

8 Items

Clearly the wording of an item has to be unambiguous, transparent and within the assumed linguistic repertoire of the test taker. But most important is the relationship between the item and the key section of the recording that contains the information to be extracted. In principle, this interaction forms part of published descriptors of test taker behaviour and/or internal instructions given to item writers. However, the type of direction given tends to be rather general and does not specify what the items should aim for in terms of the type and range of the listening processes that they elicit.

Lexical overlap

An obvious first consideration is the extent to which the wording of an item should be allowed to overlap with that of the recording. The danger is that such overlaps encourage the type of test-wise strategy (often promoted by crammer institutions as a 'key word' technique) in which a test taker attempts to map from a written word form to the same one heard in the recording. At the lowest proficiency levels and in tests designed for very young learners, this may be unexceptionable: it does after all require a degree of low-level processing in terms of input decoding. However, it is obviously best avoided at other levels – though item writers are not averse to inserting an exact word match into an incorrect multiple choice or True-False option, with a view to tripping up the shallow listener.

The general principle is that the selective type of test format should, so far as possible, feature paraphrases of the wording that occurs in the recording, precisely to discourage key-wording. But it is a principle that is sometimes more difficult to apply to constructed formats such as gap-filling (Brindley & Slatyer, 2002). As already noted, gap-filling items conventionally follow the sequence of the main points in a recording, which already provides some indication of what they might refer to. So it is essential that the paraphrases extend to most or all of the stem, even if the word or words supplied by the test taker come direct from the recording. Of course, problems may still arise if the stem triggers highly frequent but incorrect collocational associations. Elliott & Wilson (2013: 182) quote the way in which the word *density* in an IELTS gap-fill cue triggered the response *population* when the key actually referred to *traffic density.*

Item length and complexity

Item length and complexity are sometimes used as a means of increasing test difficulty. As already noted, care needs to be taken with this expedient; there is an ever present danger that reading demands will be increased without necessarily increasing listening demands. This comment particularly applies in the case of multiple-choice items, where there is a tendency for options to become longer as one moves up the proficiency scale, and for them to become much more finely differentiated. In an attempt to increase the challenge to the learner, a three-option MCQ at lower proficiency levels may be replaced by a four-option one at higher levels. All of this does, to be sure, increase the cognitive demands imposed upon the test taker; but they are *cognitive demands created by the written input that the individual has to process* rather than by the content of the recording.

Here is an example of a set of MCQ options (quoted Field, 2013: 140) which appear to have been intentionally designed to ramp up the level of difficulty for a C1 level test taker:

> *According to Peter, when he took on the role of Prospero he was*
> *   A. relieved to be playing a challenging character for a change.*
> *   B. apprehensive at having to portray so much anger on stage.*
> *   C. amused by the audience's reaction to his performance.*
> *   D. doubtful as to whether he would enjoy the experience.*

This type of item is mercifully rare in the tests of the provider concerned, but it offers any number of problems for the test taker. The item is, first of all, very wordy, with 50 words to be scanned and parsed. The propositions in the four options are very distinct from each other, so each has to be held separately in the mind while listening, with no possibility of simplifying matters by making simple contrastive connections between them. On top of that, each macro-proposition consists of three to four variables, any one of which could be nullified by a remark in the recording (for example: *relieved + play a challenging character + for a change* plus the implication that he has not played such a character recently). And then there are those treacherous adjectives of emotion and attitude, which are so easy for L2 listeners to misinterpret or to link to slightly different semantic areas in their L1. This makes for a very demanding item – but it does so in ways that primarily test the *reading* skills and *working memory* of the test taker.

Item targeting

A way of aligning test demands more closely to the listening construct is to specify the cognitive processes that items are designed to elicit at each proficiency level, taking due account of increments in processing ability as proficiency increases (see Chapter 3). A major cause for concern, however, is that test specifications and item writers' guidelines tend to list general behavioural goals without taking steps to ensure that specific processes are included that are characteristic of the proficiency level. In practice, this means that many items tend to focus on pieces of local factual information which offer obvious targets.

A case can therefore be made for what might be called *item targeting* – in other words, designing items with a view to eliciting specific processes from the test taker that are representative of skilled listening (see the cognitive profile in Chapter 1). It is also useful to ensure that roughly the same number of items in any version of a test target these particular operations, so as to ensure comparability between versions.

Here one needs to be a little more precise and accept that it is misleading to suggest that any item taps into a single level of processing. Listening is a very complex operation, and its constituent processes interact closely with each other. So, for example, an item which aims at requiring a listener to form an inference will certainly draw upon other levels of processing: it would clearly be impossible to provide an answer without engaging in the perceptual operations involved in input decoding, lexical search and parsing. So the point needs to be made that, if reference is made in these pages to an item 'targeting' a particular level of processing, *it refers to the highest level at which the item is aimed.*

Field (2013:137) suggests that items can be designed that broadly target:

- minimal phonological distinctions between words (*input decoding*)
- meaning at the level of the word or lexical chunk (*lexical search*)
- factual meaning at the level of the utterance or complete sentence (*parsing*)
- interpretive meaning at the level of the utterance (*meaning construction*)
- meaning at discourse level (*discourse construction*).

The first of these might seem peculiarly dated: it is a long while since listening assessment relied upon testing a learner's ability to distinguish minimal pairs (Weir and Vidaković, 2013). But in fact, it is not uncommon for tests at the lower levels of the proficiency range to test the ability to discriminate between like-sounding lexical items:

> *The train leaves at A. nine-fifteen. B. nine-fifty C. five-fifteen*
> *D. five-fifty*

In line with the descriptors in Chapter 3, we might expect tests at lower proficiency levels to chiefly target perceptual processes, in other words: input decoding, lexical recognition and factual information derived from parsing. By contrast, tests at the higher levels should be targeting a wide range of demanding processes which contribute to meaning and discourse construction. These might include:

- *meaning construction*: placing a piece of information in a wider context, identifying the relative importance of a piece of information, noticing the connectives that link a speaker's points, interpreting speaker attitude, drawing inferences where a speaker is not explicit, inferring pragmatic and stylistic information, inferring links between a speaker's points, resolving anaphoric reference;
- *discourse construction*: linking new information to preceding, reporting the main point of a recording, distinguishing major and minor points, recognising signals of a change of topic, recognising the overall line of argument, reporting the speaker's overall goals, noticing inconsistency, evaluating the strength of the speaker's arguments.

Field (2013: 137–9) undertook a rough sampling of item targets across tests from the Cambridge English main suite by matching the nature of the keys that were targeted against the five phases of listening identified in Chapter 1. In effect, he classified the keys as broadly phonological, lexical, factual, drawing upon contextual meaning or drawing upon an extended discourse model (e.g. across several turns of the same speaker). Clearly, the sample was a small one; but, in very general terms, the processing demands across the different levels were found to conform to the proposals just made. For example, at A2 and B1 levels, the focus was entirely on perceptual processes (decoding, lexical search and parsing). However, there were a few unexpected findings.

- There were no purely phonological-level targets (see the train time example above), even at level A2.
- There were lexical-level targets at all levels, even at C2. This seemed to be a by-product of widespread use of the gap-filling format, which requires responses of one or more words, often taken direct from the recording. What becomes more complex at higher levels is less the number of words targeted than the written frame within which the response has to be inserted.
- At level B2, there were, as expected, items requiring meaning construction (in the forms of inference and interpretation of speaker intentions) but also some very demanding items requiring the test taker to identify information that ran across a speaker's entire set of turns (i.e. information at discourse level). Curiously, there were no similar discourse-level items at C1 level, though they were well represented at C2 level.

As already stressed, the sample was a small one and some disparities in the distribution of tasks are to be expected when item writers are relying mainly on their own experience. But the findings reinforce the argument that item writer guidelines and test specifications should represent items more narrowly in terms of the cognitive processes that they aim to elicit from test takers, and should standardise the processes to be elicited at each level.

Conclusions for practice:
- Item writers should take care to avoid relying on item length and complexity as a means of increasing test difficulty, given that test items a) are in most cases delivered in written form and thus load on to reading rather than listening and b) already impose quite complex operational demands that do not correspond closely to the realities of everyday listening.
- There is a case for specifying in writers' guidelines that items within a test should target particular listening processes, taking due account of both the declared behavioural goals of the test and the level of processing of which the test taker is capable. The number of items that target each process should ideally be standardised to ensure consistency between versions of the same test.
- It is important to ensure that higher proficiency tests include an adequate number of items aimed at eliciting the types of process involved in meaning and discourse representation. This is

especially a consideration in tests that claim to measure academic or professional listening proficiency.

Item targeting at different proficiency levels

There follow some concrete recommendations for item design at various levels, which accord quite closely with the descriptors proposed in Chapter 3.

Items at lower levels up to B1+. In deciding on the types of format and item to be employed at levels up to B1, we must take account of the fact that the listener may be quite dependent upon word-level recognition and upon inferring connections between a limited number of words that have been successfully identified (usually the most perceptually prominent ones). This has consequences for item writing.

- It is reasonable that a proportion of the items target word-level keys.
- The information targeted should be mainly at a factual level and avoid inference, interpretation of speaker's intention etc.
- One area worth targeting is the ability to recognise recurrent chunks of language.
- Care should be taken not to rely upon keys which depend heavily upon function words or upon the types of relationship that are conveyed by functional expressions of low prominence (*instead of, rather than*). This consideration should also inform the use of distractors.
- However (somewhat contradicting the foregoing), it is appropriate for tests at lower levels to target, at least in some items, the *strategic competence* of the test taker. In particular, it is reasonable to ask the test taker to identify the main point of a short recording, even where the assumption is that there are parts of the recording which the test taker has been unable to decode.

Items at Level B2. It is reasonable to expect a B2 candidate to be able to handle many of the processes associated with what has been termed *meaning construction*. Items should elicit a combination of factual responses and responses that require the listener to interpret the information received or to place it within a wider context based on world knowledge etc.

- In terms of *factually-based* items: there should be a focus on more complex factual information at phrase and clause level, including information conveyed by function words of low prominence.

- In terms of *interpretation*: items can require test takers to interpret both pragmatic content and simple speaker intentions. It is reasonable to include items that focus on logical relationships conveyed by the more frequent connectives. Test takers can be asked to infer connections between adjacent utterances, and it may be useful to include items that test their ability to link pronouns and other anaphors to what they refer to. They could also be asked to compare the clearly-expressed views of two different speakers.
- In terms of *discourse level* items: test takers should be capable of reporting the general line of argument of a speaker, and placing a speaker's comments in a wider context, using world knowledge etc.
- In terms of *strategy* use, which should continue to be tested: items should target the ability to deal with unknown words. Test takers can also be expected to handle passages that may not be fully understood; here decision-making might involve choosing to infer missing information, to identify the main point or to ignore sections that are irrelevant.

Items at C level. As noted in Chapter 3, the listening behaviour of learners at CEFR levels C1 and C2 is marked by an increased ability to recognise the structure of a piece of discourse and to build up a record of that discourse point by point. At these levels, items should ideally focus upon:

- distinguishing main and subsidiary points and points which are peripheral
- recognising the links between points of information
- clearly following a line of argument
- inferring unexpressed points; inferring information from lexical cues
- recognising signposts which indicate a new direction on the part of the speaker
- recognising and comparing speakers' attitudes
- identifying and critiquing points of view
- summarising a speaker's points showing awareness of their relative importance.

Are targets necessarily met?

A case has been made for writers to design test items that aim to elicit a particular listening process from a test taker; but how sure can we be that these items do indeed produce the expected outcome? In some cases, the target is relatively clearly defined by the form of the question: *What is the main point? What is the speaker's attitude? What is the connection between [flooding] and [house building]? What two reasons does the speaker give for believing that .... Fill in the missing parts in this summary.* In other cases, however, one cannot be entirely certain that the wording of a question has been correctly interpreted and/or that the writer's intention has been realised in the behaviour adopted by the candidate.

At higher proficiency levels, this might particularly concern items where the candidate was required to form an inference (e.g. on the basis of evidence in the text or in relation to an unexpressed connection between two pieces of information). At lower levels, it might concern items that aim to target a particular type of perceptual process: e.g. extracting information at clause level or at word level, making use of intonational stress, using a particular strategy to deal with an unknown word, recognising chunks of language.

This points to the need for an additional strand of test trialling: one where we do not simply fall back on statistical evidence but try to tap in to what is going on in the mind of a test taker when faced with a draft set of items. Of course, getting that kind of evidence is neither easy nor always 100% reliable. But that is no reason for not attempting to validate items in this way, to see how they are being handled. At the very least, it provides valuable insights into test taker behaviour, including the use of test-wise strategies that thwart the intentions of the item writer.

The problem, as ever, is that listening is an internal process which leaves no traces in the way that writing and speaking do, and cannot be tracked physically in the way that reading can. So what kind of approach can one employ in order to get into the mind of a test taker while he/she is engaged in choosing answers to questions? Clearly the intervention cannot take place while the individual is doing the listening, so it has to be in the form of some kind of retrospective report. Questionnaires after a trial test administration may be easy to employ and may enable large numbers of responses to be collected. But it is very apparent that they are not a good method for this kind of validation exercise. They are vulnerable to over-reporting; and their wording is prone to lead respondents to lay claim to behaviour that they did not actually engage in. Check-list questionnaires about whether respondents did or did not engage in particular perceptual processes are especially meaningless. Clearly, *all listening* engages the three perceptual levels so it makes no sense to ask learners if they are employing them – only if they are aware of problems with them.

The best way of checking whether items are hitting their targets (and more generally of investigating test taker behaviour) is to obtain verbal reports. They too are subject to certain constraints, however. Test takers have to be interviewed as soon as possible after taking the test, to ensure that they do not conjure up false memories. Even better is to divide a four-minute recording into three and interview the test taker after each section. A second important consideration is to use the item as a stimulus by specifically asking: *What answer did you give? How did you arrive at it?* General impressions can be collected at the end.

This kind of approach to validating the content of a text produces richer information than statistics can, and provides useful insights into test behaviour (see e.g. Field's (2012a) cognitive review of the IELTS lecture-listening section). A rare example of the approach being used specifically to investigate whether items hit their targets is a recent study of the Aptis Listening test by Holzknecht et al. (2017). They supported the verbal reports they obtained with eye-tracking evidence of how the test takers viewed the written items on the computer screen. Their claim that this exercise cognitively validates the Aptis test is wide of the mark: the processes studied relate to the world of the test rather than the real world. But the information provides useful insights into the way in which candidates respond to the challenges set by different types of test item target.

LISTENER ROLES

9 Special cases

The discussion so far has been largely concerned with tests of general L2 listening aimed at adults. However, tests also have to be designed with more specific populations in mind – including those who listen under special conditions and those whose level of cognitive development shapes the type of listening they can engage in. If such tests are to accurately predict performance in real-world conditions, they need to take full account of the contexts in which these learners encounter the second language, the type of spoken input they encounter, how they handle that input and/or any limitations that may restrict what can be demanded of them. This chapter will consider two of these special groups of listeners: namely those needing L2 listening for academic purposes and those acquiring the skill at a young age. These populations are quite distinct. In the first case, the major issue is the context within which the test taker will be operating and the nature of the listening task. In the second, it is the limitations upon what it is reasonable to expect by way of listening behaviour.

Up to now, the discussion has also taken for granted the conventional single-skill test of listening. Chapter 10 goes on to explore the practicality of using tests that combine listening with other L2 skills. A particular consideration there will be the extent to which integrated-skills tests can be said to replicate the types of real-world activity in which specific groups of listeners would be expected to engage.

Academic listeners

It is worth noting that, in his early proposals for listening 'sub-skills', Richards (1983) proposed two separate groups: one for general listening and one for academic listening. Despite that, we still lack a sufficiently detailed account of what the academic listening experience entails. The major considerations in designing valid tests for this population must be:
- to represent as closely as possible the type of spoken input that academic listeners encounter.
- to create tasks and items that elicit as closely as possible the cognitive processes that they have to employ.

What types of listening event?

As part of an IELTS study, Ingram & Bayliss (2007) provided a valuable insight into what academic listeners actually do during the course of their studies – valuable because it is underpinned by reports obtained from learners. The researchers asked participants across several different disciplines to specify the types of academic activity in which they principally engaged. Of the 14 pursuits the participants mentioned (p. 7), seven directly entail listening:

- Listening and note-taking
- Following spoken instructions
- Group discussions / tutorials
- Attending and giving oral presentations
- One-to-one meetings
- Working with others in a laboratory
- Practical experience working with L1 speakers.

They embody a range of different roles for the listener, both individual and interactional. Clearly a test cannot represent all of these contexts, and some are in any case quite specific to certain disciplines. A more general account might suggest that the following activities are central to most academic experience:

Lectures and presentations > Seminars > Advice and instructions > Social activities

The first two are the most critical when planning test content. Lecture-based material should ideally reflect the characteristics of good presentational style (see Chapter 6):

- Monologue mode
- Paced delivery, with medium speech rate and rhythmic intonation patterns
- Clear signalling of changes of sub-topic and summations of points made so far
- A degree of repetition, exemplification and rephrasing.

By contrast, seminar-related samples of speech should ideally feature:

- Dialogue mode (seminar leader and participant)
- Pragmatic language (inviting an opinion, expressing a view uncontentiously)

- Two different viewpoints which the test taker might be asked to differentiate.

It is obviously necessary to make use of recorded samples that are much shorter than their real-world lecture and seminar equivalents; but they should nevertheless represent discourse patterns that are as close as possible to those of actual events. In addition, one should not, even at this level, rule out the possibility of using recordings in the form of clips of around 30 seconds which represent critical moments in a presentation where a speaker (e.g.) signals a change of topic, contrasts two views or summarises a point. It is by no means uncommon, in a lecture context, for wider problems of comprehension to arise as the result of a failure to pick up local points and markers of direction.

What topics and discourse patterns?

Topic poses a dilemma for anyone attempting verisimilitude in tests of academic listening. In a real-world situation, the L2 student is a privileged listener in the sense of having a degree of familiarity with the subject area being discussed. Their access to background information and specialist terminology thus serves to compensate for gaps of understanding. This situation self-evidently cannot be replicated in a test. Instead, the test designer has to draw upon issues of debate or relatively esoteric pieces of information which test takers are *unlikely* to have encountered.

It is nonetheless possible to adopt a range of discourse types which resemble those of academic lectures. Expository and discursive material are clearly the most appropriate, both with a clear argument structure that the listener needs to follow. However, the general term 'discursive' does not really do justice to the types of discourse that an academic listener might need to handle. Reviewing a range of recordings at C level, Field (2012b) proposed the following categories as appropriate for academic contexts (though there must inevitably be some variation between disciplines):

- Expository (including cause-and-effect and counterfactual relationships)
- Discursive (weighing evidence 'for and against')
- Argumentative (putting forward a single viewpoint)
- Persuasive (trying to win the listener over)
- Analytical/interpretive (common in humanities subjects)
- Process-descriptive (Brown & Yule, 1983), featuring (e.g.) objects that potentially change their form as part of a process.

This is not to suggest that a single recording will necessarily be restricted to one of these discourse types; it may well alternate between two or more, with one type predominating.

What processes should items target?

The framework outlined in Chapter 1 identified five operations that contribute to listening. Of these, success in academic listening is especially dependent upon those at the higher levels – namely, meaning construction (interpreting significance) and discourse construction (following a line of argument). Students listening to an academic presentation need to be capable of:

- identifying the current main point
- judging whether a new piece of information is central, secondary or irrelevant
- distinguishing macro-propositions from micro-
- linking points of information (especially where the links have to be inferred)
- integrating new information into a developing discourse representation
- monitoring the developing discourse representation for consistency
- building an overall discourse structure which represents the lecturer's line of argument.

Processing at the levels of meaning and discourse is often curiously under-represented in the testing of L2 academic listening. Item writers tend to focus on interesting points of information, with the consequence that their items target a string of isolated facts, without requiring test takers to report the wider argument that links them. There is no reason, however, (see Chapter 8) why emphasis should not be placed on items that elicit specific processes like those in the list above.

What task formats to use?

The use of a *gap-filling* format might seem an obvious option in an academic context, on the grounds that it resembles the type of note-taking that an academic listener does during a lecture. In fact, the analogy does not quite hold true: in a test, the notes are the work of somebody other than the student and are read in advance of hearing the recording. Of course, the very demanding metacognitive activity of co-ordinating three skills under pressures of time does have some important parallels with the real-world student experience of having to read PP slides and take notes while at the same time listening to the lecturer's voice.

That said, gap-filling possesses one major disadvantage in an academic listening context. As suggested earlier, the need to select short responses of around three words encourages item writers to choose simple keys in the text at the level of the word or phrase; so the format is better suited to the reporting of facts than to reporting larger connections. One way of adapting the conventional gap-fill to fit academic needs more closely is to present the task in the form of a Table of Contents outline of the recorded material, with just the occasional heading or sub-heading supplied. Test takers can be asked to supply the missing entries, and thus in effect to supply a summary of what they have heard, showing the extent to which they have been able to recognise discourse-level patterns of argument.

The *multiple-choice* format is in some ways more flexible, and enables items to elicit a wider range of the relevant processes listed above. However, the earlier warning about loading difficulty on to written MCQ options still holds. Distinguishing between complex propositions is indeed part of the competence needed to study at an academic institution; but it needs to be tested by the recorded content and not by the written items. Perhaps the most useful of the conventional formats in academic contexts is *multiple-matching*, which is usually more economical in terms of the amount and complexity of the reading required. It lends itself well to tasks where candidates identify points made or not made by a speaker or contrast the viewpoints of two speakers.

The comments so far apply to large-scale tests where easy and reliable marking is an issue. For more local tests (say in EAP language centres), the best way of measuring academic listening proficiency is simply to ask test takers to make bullet-pointed notes of what they hear and to check them on a second play, when they might also identify and underline major headings. Raters need to agree on the number of major and minor propositions in a text and match them against those that a candidate reports. Clearly this introduces a note of subjectivity into the testing process; but, positively, it avoids the need for a written pre-presented question sheet and the inevitable test-wise strategies that ensue. In a study of the lecture-based section of the IELTS test, nearly 30% of participants (N = 26) stated emphatically that they found free note-taking less arduous than the complexities of obeying a standard test format (Field, 2012a: 422).

Can we replicate the lecture context?

In the real world, academic listeners have access to cues other than the voice of the lecturer. As just noted, competence in real-world lecture listening (whether in L1 or L2) involves a complex process of mapping between written words on a PP slide and the points that the speaker is making. In point of fact, this operation is not as easy for the aspiring L2 listener as it might appear. Most experienced lecturers avoid simply reading aloud what appears on the slides. Instead, they use the text as a trigger to memory and then go on to paraphrase it and/or to elaborate on it. In other words, one important mark of academic listening competence is the ability to *map from written words to paraphrase and vice versa*. Yet this is something that is rarely if ever tested within tests, whether international or local. In computer-delivered versions, it should surely be possible in at least one section of a test to simulate the lecture situation more closely by accompanying the speaker's voice with summative PP slides.

Young Learners

The discussion here will be limited to YLs of primary ages. On present evidence, we can make broad generalisations about the patterns of development of younger learners (Goswami, 1998, 2006, Meadows, 2006), but it is much more difficult to trace consistent patterns in those of 12 to 16, who vary enormously both in the ways in which they develop cognitively and in the rate at which they develop (Blakemore, 2007).

Young listeners represent a very different case from academic ones. A test developer does indeed need to take full account of the domains within which they operate and the forms of L2 that they are likely to need to use. But a major area of concern must be the test takers' level of development in terms of the cognitive processes that they employ in order to make sense of second language speech. The providers of listening tests in this area make considerable efforts to adapt their content to the interests of young learners, the L2 lexical fields that they are likely to have been introduced to and the contexts with which they are familiar. But they tend to give rather less attention to the fact that their target test takers can be expected to operate cognitively in ways that are markedly different from those of an adult.

What makes young listeners cognitively different?

Young listeners are still in the process of acquiring certain important cognitive functions. Between the ages of 5 and 12, children exhibit distinctive behaviour in terms of:

- *working memory capacity.* Their more limited working memory restricts the amount of information they can store in the mind at any given time.
- *metacognitive control.* More limited control over mental operations affects young listeners' ability to choose techniques appropriate to a task; to switch attention between sources of information; and to collate incoming information so as to make informed and rapid decisions.
- *logical reasoning.* Up to 11 or 12 years old, young listeners have difficulty in recognising inconsistency and ambiguity, forming and testing hypotheses or following ideas that are counter to reality *(If it had rained, I'd have stayed at home).*
- *inferencing.* Young listeners find it difficult to make inferences about points of information that a speaker has not expressed explicitly. This may reflect the way their minds operate; or it may be the result of more limited world knowledge or more limited understanding of how pragmatic language functions.

For a detailed review of the capabilities of young listeners and their implications for test design see Field (2018).

It would seem that designers of L2 listening tests for Young Learners are well advised to focus principally on the perceptual operations described in Chapter 3 (input decoding, lexical search and parsing). Items which demand higher-level processes such as making inferences on the basis of world knowledge, reporting a line of argument or interpreting speaker intentions are likely to be beyond the cognitive competence of many YLs of 10 and under. Extensive research into L1 comprehension skills by Oakhill and colleagues, much of it based upon read-aloud texts, suggests three particular areas of difficulty for YL comprehenders: inferencing, self-monitoring and following discourse markers (Yuill & Oakhill, 1998). The research also highlights problems in linking pronouns to the words they refer back to, particularly when there is a time lapse between the two.

Unsurprisingly (given their more limited metacognitive control), the indications are that YLs are not as strategically oriented as adults. They are likely to find most types of compensatory strategy demanding in that they entail assessing a problem, identifying possible solutions and then choosing between them. Recorded material should therefore be as explicit as possible, with caution exercised about language that candidates may not know. In one particular area of strategy use, however, YLs might well find themselves competent: namely working out the meanings of unfamiliar words from their immediate co-text, something they have been doing from their very first L1 speech encounters.

What recorded content is appropriate?

With these considerations in mind, a number of conclusions can be drawn about the type of test content most suitable for young listeners. Some of them represent what is already quite common practice; the point here is to argue whether they do or do not reflect the cognitive realities of the population that is targeted.

Let us first consider the *recording as text*. Narratives, instructions and clearly-signposted descriptions are the most appropriate discourse types, for reasons already cited in relation to lower proficiency adults: namely their use of simple chronological or physical sequences. The topics and contexts featured obviously need to be familiar, with no unrealistic expectations about the test taker's world knowledge. This is rather more complicated than it sounds in the case of international tests, since there are inevitably large cultural variations among different populations. Item writers sometimes try to get round the problem and at the same time appeal to the imagination of YLs by using fantasy situations. However, this approach needs to be handled with care. Young learners are sometimes quite surprisingly commonsense in their interpretations (Donaldson, 2006: 88–90) and inclined to rationalise both counter-intuitive situations and counter-intuitive questions (e.g. *Is the table under the book?*).

YL test providers are sensitive to the need to limit the length of the recordings used and thus their information load. They often exercise a preference for short clips rather than longer recordings. The advantage of the clip is that there is usually just one question per recording so that the young listener is spared the uncertainty of having to hold two or more questions in working memory in case a key has been missed. A less recognised precept is that it is also advisable to monitor the length of the *utterances*. It will be recalled that a listener has to store most or all of an utterance in the mind in order to parse it for syntax. Long utterances therefore place heavy demands upon younger listeners, given their working memory limitations. To ensure that any guidelines upon utterance length are fully applied at the time of recording, a good policy is to mark utterance boundaries on actors' scripts.

Care also needs to be taken to control the density and complexity of information, so that the young test taker is not required to identify and link too many ideas. In dialogues, information can be thinned out by Q&A patterns which enable part of the information to be delivered via the question and part via the answer. However, some of the more obvious ways of relieving information load should be handled with care. For example, scripts where speakers repeat points by rephrasing them oblige the young listener to make decisions as to whether they are hearing a repeated point or a new one.

So far as the *recording as speech* is concerned, a mixture of monologue and dialogue material seems appropriate. Listening tests designed for young EFL non-immersion learners often make much use of the latter; but sometimes overlook the part played by monologues in primary classroom listening materials, in the form of stories, basic instructions, descriptive texts and songs.

We noted previously that normalising to unfamiliar voices is a multi-faceted operation which adults take for granted in an L1 context. It can be a demanding one for younger listeners, especially where L2 adult voices are concerned. Instead of providing a wide variety of voices across an L2 listening test in the belief that it will sustain interest and motivation, providers do better to limit the number of actors used. So far as local tests of progress and achievement are concerned, the best resource is possibly the voice of the teacher, which is not only the most important source of L2 for learners, but represents the local variety of English. Also with regard to adjusting to voices – the L1 accent used in test recordings should be the one to which learners have been most exposed i.e. the variety of English that features in the national curriculum. (See the discussion in Chapter 5 about how accent familiarity is acquired.) Allowance must be made for the difficulty that YLs experience in dealing with ambivalent information, here in the form of vowel variations in the signal.

What task formats to use?

Using unmodified conventional test formats with young test takers is problematic. There are two major issues: a) the fact that these formats rely upon items in written form when (at least in the lower age ranges) even L1 reading skills may still be evolving; and b) the fact that these adult formats demand cognitive processes that add considerably to the difficulty of the task.

So far as the written modality is concerned, it is obviously important to keep items short and simple. In local tests, it makes sense to formulate the questions in the first language. This not only ensures that items are more likely to be understood; it also eliminates any temptation to engage in test-wise strategies based on key words – something that (see above) YLs may in any case not be very good at. An alternative solution is to make extensive use of visuals to reduce reading demands. Typical formats include: large visuals accompanied by oral questions about what they show or statements to be verified; maps and plans on which directions have to be traced or sections labelled; pictures which have to be placed in order.

A more intractable problem lies in the complex processes unrelated to the listening skill that conventional formats elicit. While multiple-choice is quite often favoured in YL tests, the task demands not only careful reading skills but also precisely the kind of option-evaluating, decision-making operation that YLs find difficult. The demands of the test are thus heavily weighted on to the task rather than the listening experience. One solution is to make use of visual MCQs (see the description in Chapter 6). Another is to restrict the options to three and to ensure that they are short (2 to 3 words) and that they are distinctive (*red, yellow, blue* rather than *often, usually, sometimes*).

Gap-filling is also demanding for young learners because (as already noted) it entails a divided-attention situation and thus a great deal of meta-cognitive control in switching between reading, listening and writing. At lower levels and younger ages, it is advisable to keep the frames very simple (e.g. completing notices and lists), and to limit the words to be inserted to a maximum of (say) two. One variation provides learners with a transcript of the recorded material where gaps replace a number of the words, and thus narrowly tests the ability to decode and make lexical matches. In computer-delivered tests, it may be possible to introduce a drag-and-drop labelling task which restricts the amount of reading that needs to be done.

What to target?

It was suggested above that items should largely target perceptual processes. At the lowest levels, this might include the simple recognition of words, either in isolation or within a piece of connected speech. More generally keys in a recording might be found at the level of the word, the phrase or the clause. There is sometimes an inclination for YL tests to target the knowledge of language rather than the extraction of meaning; this should be avoided in tests of listening; and sight should not be lost of the auditory side of the whole exercise. That means that, if vocabulary is the focus, it is more relevant at low levels to test the ability to identify like-sounding words than words belonging to a single lexical set. Particular care is needed so far as targeting specific points of grammar is concerned. YLs are often not adept at acquiring explicit grammar knowledge; but they do have the facility to recognise and acquire recurrent chunks of language (Wray, 2001). Another consideration is that some of the commonest linguistic features (particularly function words) are of relatively low prominence in connected speech and hard to recognise. Prepositions of position, much favoured in YL tests, sometimes fall into this category.

Further special cases

Test providers and testing researchers have given depressingly little attention to the situation of those who, at primary or early secondary level, are being tested for their readiness to move on to learning through the medium of English. This population has very particular needs that combine those of the two groups we have considered so far. Like academic listeners, they need to be capable of listening to a combination of monologue presentations and whole-class discussions; but like other young listeners, they face constraints on how much they can process, given, especially at primary level, their evolving metacognitive skills.

For this group, listening is not a take-it-or-leave-it option. It is the key to their future lives and careers. It they enter EMI unable to follow what the teacher is saying to them, then their education will be lost and with it their futures. They face the prospect of anything between three and seven years spent sitting in classrooms surrounded by alien sounds, with the only lifeline being to try to extract written information from a blackboard or a coursebook. There is a very real issue here in defining the specific needs of this group so that tests can be devised that validly and reliably measure their ability to perform the type of listening that will be required of them before they move on to EMI.

A parallel situation can be found in the testing of L2 listening skills in relation to professional needs. General tests of L2 listening, or tests designed chiefly to measure academic English, are widely used in order to determine an individual's ability to perform in a number of professional contexts. Target scores in these tests are used as criteria for immigration or feature in job specifications cited by employers. The tests in question may roughly serve their purpose where the posts require the applicant to be capable of performing adequately in routine work situations (taking instructions, listening to colleagues, understanding work routines) – though admittedly it is difficult to see how listening to a lecture relates to any work-based experience other than attending a presentation. The major concern is that there exist a number of occupations which require very specific forms of listening or listening that has to be extremely accurate. They include airline pilots, simultaneous translators, engineers, police officers and even call centre operators (tested for their speaking skills but rarely for the ability to comprehend any but the most predictable questions).

Perhaps of greatest concern is that they include medical professionals. A major research project in this area was undertaken by Berry, O'Sullivan & Rugea (2013) on behalf of the UK General Medical Council (GMC). It consulted 62 participants across 7 geographical locations, and the 11 panels included five types of stakeholder: medical directors, doctors, nurses, allied health professionals and (often overlooked in such studies) patients. During the panel discussions, the participants were asked to brainstorm the characteristics that they thought a minimally competent candidate should possess, and to complete two IELTS listening tests in order to record how many questions from each a minimally qualified candidate should be expected to answer. The approach thus encouraged panellists to focus on language skills and behavioural evidence within their own professional fields – particularly where patient safety might be an issue.

One of the more striking findings related to listening, which all the panels rated of high importance for their work context. They unanimously recommended a score band of 8.5 (as compared with 7.5 for the other three skills). As one panel participant put it (p.69): 'Listening is the key … Most of [our] communication is about listening and taking in the information and particularly in the patient setting'. However, an alternative (or complementary) explanation for advocating such a high target score is that the test was perceived as relatively easy. A number of panellists expressed this view, while others questioned the extent to which, either in content or in tasks, the test represented the types of communication that a doctor or nurse would need to engage in.

Another study by Sedgwick, Garner and Vicente-Macia (2016) focused specifically on nurses. It too bears witness to the mismatch between the entry requirements for the British National Health Service (at the time, an IELTS score of 7) and the complex listening and note-taking tasks in which nurses have to engage (including a need for considerable socio-pragmatic competence).

The findings quoted provide telling examples of the issues that arise when tests mainly devised for academic gatekeeping are employed as the basis for determining whether test takers are capable of operating in a specific professional environment. It is not simply a matter of the way terminology and discourse patterns vary across the different contexts. It is also a question of considerable differences in the way in which speech is employed to receive and communicate information. The conclusion reached by Berry at al. was that IELTS should be treated by medical administrators as a filter to test general aptitude in English and should then be followed by a test like the GMC's PLAB that is more specific to the language and the contexts that applicants are going to encounter in real-world work situations. But of course, any such test entails a complex process of co-operation between those who are expert in testing and those with no linguistic background but familiar with the circumstances of the workplace.

An interesting precedent of a test designed specifically with medical contexts in mind is to be found in the Occupational English Test (OET) used by the Australian health service for overseas applicants. However, the problem that arises there is that the test is aimed at all health professionals. This is particularly an issue in the case of the listening paper. Its heavy task demands (including relatively rapid speech and an extremely high level of item density) do not represent the conditions that, for example, a nurse might have to deal with. This example suggests the need for even greater specificity in both content and task parameters if we are to design tests that validly represent the listening needs of distinct professional groups.

10 Listening plus other skills

Tests of oral communication

While listening is often tested in isolation, it is also implicated in any test attempting to measure spoken communication between individuals. In tests of L2 Speaking, visuals are sometimes used to generate candidate performance, but in most cases what the candidate says is in response to oral input of some kind – brief or extended, live or recorded – from another speaker. A number of recent studies of examiner-candidate exchanges (e.g. May, 2007, Galaczi 2010, Nakatsuhara, 2012) have drawn attention to the importance of listening as part of the interaction that takes place.

This raises difficult questions: How critical are candidates' listening skills to their ability to perform in a test that purportedly measures speaking? And to what extent is the score assigned by an examiner indirectly influenced by the candidate's ability to understand and respond relevantly to what is said? One answer is that much depends upon the goals that are set for the test. If the test provider has characterised it as a test of *Speaking* and there is a separate test to assess listening skills, then the problem lies in whether and how one can eliminate listening from the criteria used by the assessor, or at least downgrade it. On the other hand, if the test is specifically characterised as a test of *Interactive communication*, then listening must surely contribute to the final score, and the question becomes: To what extent?

The situation is complicated even further in tests which have a three-way structure, where the candidate has to interact, not only with the examiner but also with a fellow student. Nakatsuhara (2011) reports that communication problems in group tests may be attributable in part to limited listening proficiency. But to what extent should we take into account the candidate's ability to understand not simply an L1 speaker in the person of the examiner but also a fellow L2 speaker? A generalised answer to this question is impossible given that the latter may be familiar as a classmate, familiar in terms of the L2 variety of English that he/she speaks or entirely unfamiliar on both counts (see the earlier discussion of potential bias caused by accent). Ducasse &

Brown (2009) provide evidence of the way in which paired candidates support each other's listening by supplying missing words and back-channelling; but the issue remains of what importance should be attached to *failures of comprehension* between candidates.

There are no easy answers to the questions that have been raised; but a study by Nakatsuhara and Field (2012) sheds a little light on what occurs in face-to-face encounters. It investigated the performance of 20 examiners in a Trinity College Graded Examination in Spoken English, specifically designated as a test of *interactive communication*. The goal was to investigate the nature of the support provided by examiners and the extent to which listening skills appeared to contribute to the score awarded. Some limited evidence was found of examiners modifying their language to reflect an instinctive judgement, made quite early on, as to the listening skills of the candidate. Interestingly, though, there were also a few instances where examiners seemed not to take account of the accuracy of candidates' listening and awarded scores mainly or entirely on the basis of the fluency of their speech productions. In one case in particular, the examiner graded a candidate at the top level. However, a close analysis of the transcript suggested that the candidate had under-stood few of the requests that the examiner had made but had managed to produce an apparently fluent piece of discourse that was not entirely relevant and possibly pre-rehearsed.

The solution recommended, and put into practice, was firstly to provide training to raise examiners' awareness of listening as an important con-tributory factor in examiner-candidate exchanges. Secondly, as this was specifically a test of communication, the rating criteria were expanded to include listening as a separate scored category alongside Communication skills, Grammar, Lexis and Phonology (in effect, giving Listening a 20% weighting).

But the wider conclusions to be drawn are that experienced oral examin-ers may not always be as sensitive to the part played by listening as they are to evidence of fluency of speech delivery. Candidates should perhaps also be given credit, not simply for the accuracy of their listening, but also for the way in which they deal strategically with any breakdowns of understanding that occur. What is unfortunate here is that one very obvi-ous indicator– the time taken to respond to an examiner's turn – is very ambivalent. A delayed response may mark a problem of listening, or it may mark a problem in assembling what to say.

Listening into...

Following the recent development of reading-into-writing tasks, there has been speculation about the practicality of pairing listening with other skills in order to assess the candidate's ability to transfer information from one form to another. Any serious consideration of the idea has to accept the reality that mixed-skills testing must inevitably blur the boundary between the information derived from listening and how successfully that information is subsequently handled. The effect is to considerably reduce the extent to which a test can provide reliable evidence of an individual's listening proficiency – evidence that may be critical in entry tests, progress tests or classroom-based tests seeking weaknesses for remedial practice. Three other perspectives on this issue also need to be taken into account: an ecological one (how likely is this type of information transfer to happen in the real world?), a cognitive one (what are the precise demands of the operation?) and a practical one (how easy it is to arrive at a reliable score?)

Listening into writing

From an ecological perspective, the most obvious candidate is listening into writing, given that listeners sometimes need to make notes of what they hear in order to assist later recall. This type of activity is associated with a number of real-world situations and very specific types of discourse: one thinks of students taking notes from lectures, the police interviewing witnesses, minute takers, general listeners writing down instructions or noting times, dates and addresses given in phone calls. What this means is that full account may need to be taken of precisely how relevant listening-into-writing is likely to be to the target population, One also has to ensure that the recorded material used is of a kind that is likely to give rise to the need for a written record.

Of greater concern is the fact that both listening and writing are cognitively very complex activities. Any combination of the two must inevitably give rise to divided attention effects, with the candidate having to simultaneously co-ordinate two modalities and two sets of processes. These effects are especially a factor to be considered at lower proficiency levels, where substantial effort has to be given to word recognition and to the generation of correct word forms and spellings. As for scoring, there is clearly a tension between the ability to decode words and utterances in a spoken modality and the ability to render them accurately in a written one. What, for example, should be the penalties attached to incorrect grammar or spelling?

Listening into reading

Ecologically, the combination of listening with reading might appear relevant in an EAP context, where it can be said to replicate the process of combining information from oral and written sources that forms part of academic study. In this case, it makes sense for the information provided by the two sources to be markedly different so that the task of the test taker is clearly accretional (combining and connecting two separate sets of information) or contrastive (comparing two different viewpoints). This might then enable testers to score for individual skills as well as for the performance of the task as a whole. The compiled information would presumably have to be tested by means of conventional comprehension questions, though more demanding ones than normal in that they would need to switch between sources.

From a cognitive perspective, there are certainly a few concerns. There might be memory effects if a time-constrained listening passage was followed by a time-rich reading activity. If note-taking were used in order to compensate for this, there would again be divided attention effects. In addition, it would need to be clearly acknowledged that the task measures a level of cognitive competence (namely the integration of information) that, though relevant to an EAP candidate, goes beyond a purely language-based skill.

Listening into speaking

The task here differs from the interactive situation discussed in the previous section in that it requires the transfer of information from one source to another without an interlocutor. In ecological terms, this appears to be the least likely of the three combinations. Granted, there are a few circumstances in which the combination would occur. It could be claimed to replicate the way a listener acquires facts or instructions with a view to passing them on. In an EAP context, it might also be said to replicate the way in which information from a lecture or seminar might later inform a student's own oral presentation. This appears to have been the rationale behind including the format in a revision of the TOEFL listening test. However, the practice of rewarding the ability to report lecture content in a way that follows the source so closely and adds nothing seems unlikely to meet the approval of real-world academics. What is more: the ecological argument does not quite add up. Students preparing a presentation would surely draw upon reading sources, as much if not more than material derived from lecture notes. In fact, if lecture notes failed to stimulate a sufficiently clear recall of what was said, they would almost certainly fall back on sources that were more reliable – following the natural instinct of L2 users to trust permanent written sources more than transitory spoken ones.

There is also a scoring issue for this format. To what extent should one reward a presentation that reproduced almost the exact form of words used in the listening phase? Listeners in some cultures have excellent memories for the words they hear and it is by no means impossible that they could repeat at least some of them verbatim without having fully integrated them into a meaningful account. The likelihood is increased if note-taking is allowed with a view to avoiding memory effects – thus giving the candidate the opportunity to note down words and chunks of language ahead of the speaking phase. In these instances, the test might, at least in part, end up simply measuring word- and phrase-level recognition.

Conclusions for practice:
With all these caveats in mind, the conclusion has to be that while 'listening into…' formats might appear to present an alternative to more conventional comprehension-based approaches, they are hard to justify in terms of the argument that they represent real-world processes of information transfer. They are very complex in cognitive terms, demanding behaviour that extends well beyond what is associated with a single skill – and the outputs are in general uninformative in terms of precisely where errors may have arisen. One possible exception may be where tests are designed for candidates with special requirements (academic or professional) which to some extent override the need to assess skills individually. The issue of academic listening and note-taking is perhaps a special case: notes are by their nature rough and are unlikely ever to be assessed in terms of an individual's writing skills, though they can certainly provide valuable insights into accuracy of listening.

POSTSCRIPT

11 Information load: an investigative study

Among the aspects of recording-as-text discussed in Chapter 4 was the idea that text length necessarily contributes to test difficulty. It was suggested there that what makes a longer recording more difficult may not be the attentional demands of listening for 3 to 5 minutes but the greater information load that the listener has to handle. Indeed, length may not always be a determining factor. In principle, a long recording might be relatively simple to process if it contained a great deal of repetition and rephrasing and was thus low on the quantity of information to be retrieved. Conversely, it is possible to have a demanding short recording in which many critical points are made in a limited period of time.

Information density and information complexity have been little discussed in the L2 listening literature. Clearly, both are an issue for listeners who have to build detailed discourse representations of what they hear. The more information that needs to be processed in a listening passage, the more demanding it is to construct a clear line of argument. Similarly, the process of building up a clear line of argument becomes more demanding if there are complex links between the various points of information.

This chapter focuses particularly upon information density. At the outset, it is worth noting that the term is sometimes used rather vaguely, without a full appreciation of the implications for test design. In fact there are three very distinct ways in which an item writer might increase information load when attempting to control the difficulty of the scripts in a listening test.

    a. By extending the length of a recording (in effect, increasing the number of pieces of information to be assimilated)

    b. By concentrating more and more points of information into the same number of words (in effect, increasing the intensity of the information to be assimilated)

    c. By increasing the number of words that it takes to assemble a point of information (in effect, increasing the elaborateness of the information)

The distinction is important in terms of the impact upon the test taker. The first two approaches increase the difficulty of *building a discourse-level representation*. In the first, *more* has to be integrated into the speaker's line of argument. In the second, the information has to be integrated *faster*. The third approach affects the demands of *parsing*: more words have to be held in the mind per piece of information derived.

A previous study

A rare attempt to measure information density and complexity across proficiency levels (Field, 2013: 121–125) formed part of a recent review of the Cambridge English listening tests. Field drew upon Chafe's (1979) notion of an *idea unit*, a unit of meaning in the mind[1]. On the basis of evidence from oral narrative material, Chafe (1980) asserted that in natural speech a typical unit of this kind was

- likely to correspond to a single unit of intonation, preceded and followed by some form of planning pause;
- likely to be represented linguistically by a single clause constructed around a Verb Phrase.

Chafe went on to relate these two characteristics to the psychology of the speaker – in particular to limitations on how much information can be held in the mind at any one time as the basis for an utterance.

Field (2013) analysed the short clips used in Section 1 of sample Cambridge English tests at PET, FCE and CPE levels. The clips targeted three different CEFR proficiency bands (respectively, B1, B2 and C2). His hypothesis was that there would be a gradual increase in the number and density of idea units across levels, and thus in the cognitive demands associated with building a line of argument. Following Chafe, he used the presence of a finite verb as a rule-of-thumb marker of an idea unit (IU), regardless of whether the verb occurred in a main clause or a subordinate one. Phatic language and uninformative content such as greetings or back channelling were ignored. This made possible a calculation of the average number of pieces of information in the passages, which were shown to increase from 11.71 at PET level (range 10–13) to 14.25 at FCE level (range 12–16) and then on to 22.00 (range 18–26) at CPE. Here, there appeared to be clear evidence of an increase in the information load

---

[1] This term was preferred to Bachman's (1990) *propositional unit* on the grounds that the word *proposition* is associated in Semantics with abstract, context-free information.

as the proficiency level increased (the first possibility mentioned above) – though the effect was, of course, partly the outcome of the way the texts increased in length, in terms of both words and duration.

The question then was how to calculate the actual density of these information units within a text. An obvious solution was to divide the length of the text in words by the number of units (thus producing figures for 'words per IU') and the length of the text in time by the number of units (thus producing figures for 'seconds per IU'). Similarly, the amount of subordination in the texts (and thus the level of syntactic complexity) was measured by comparing the number of main clauses to the number of IUs. The figures below show the mean values for the clips studied.

	Mean IUs	Mean Words per IU	Mean Secs. per IU	Mean IUs per Main Verb
PET (A2)	11.71 (10–13)	6.92	2.40	1.49 (0.34)
FCE (B2)	14.25 (12–16)	7.36	2.14	1.74 (0.30)
CPE (C2)	22.00 (18–26)	8.70	2.64	1.84 (0.24)

Last column figures in brackets indicate SDs

Table 3: Density and embeddedness of idea units in Part 1 recordings of three tests

There appeared to be a clear effect of proficiency level on the number of words per IU, which increased as the passages became more demanding. Something similar is true for the duration of the IUs, if one allows for the use of slowed speech at PET level. This points to the third scenario mentioned at the outset. *When item writers wished to raise the difficulty of a script, they increased the number of words that had to be processed in order to access an IU – thus making parsing more demanding.* The figures in the final column also suggest that, as proficiency rises, an increasingly large number of idea units is to be found in subordinate as well as main clauses.

The study just described begs a number of questions. Firstly, it examined only a limited sample of texts across three different tests; it was of interest to see if the findings could be confirmed elsewhere. Secondly, it relied on a rough measure of information density based on counting finite verbs. If this proved to be a reliable measure, then the way would be open to using a computer programme to automatically measure how many idea units there were in a script by means of a simple verb count. If it did not, then any test designer who wanted to use information density as a factor in deciding the difficulty of a listening text would need a set of relatively precise specifications as to how to identify an IU. And, if such guidelines could indeed be provided, how likely was it that different item writers would be able to use them consistently in evaluating draft scripts?

The present exercise

With these questions in mind, the present study explored the practicality of measuring information density and the extent to which it is used by item writers as a means of grading the listening demands of test material across a proficiency range. The investigators were John Field (JF), author of the original study, and John Tucker (JT), team leader for British Council item writers working on the Aptis listening test. They set themselves three major questions:

1. Is it possible to specify clearly what does or does not constitute a point of information in a listening passage?
2. Is it possible to write up the criteria in a way that enables two raters to reach agreement when measuring information density across several recording scripts?
3. Do sample materials produced by an experienced item writer display a graded increase in information density as they progress up the proficiency scale?

Defining information units

With a view to establishing how difficult it is to define an IU, the two researchers reviewed a number of short sample scripts. These came from a large set of such materials, prepared for the British Council as possible future models for the Aptis listening test. The original writer of the scripts in question (JF) had targeted them at proficiency levels from A2 to C1 with no foreknowledge that they would later be subject to an investigation of their information density. The levels at which the recorded material and associated test items actually scored had subsequently been established by a trialling project undertaken by the British Council that involved 180 participants in two locations (India and China). The examples that follow in Appendix B have been drawn from these scripts.

It was quickly evident that two basic criteria from Chafe (1980) served quite consistently to identify IUs in the material.

a.   The clearest indicator was a **full verb** (regardless of tense or aspectual markers and whether in a main or subordinate clause).

That said, an analyst using this criterion has to be alert to cases of embedding: *walking the streets [if you're blind or partially sighted] can be a pretty dangerous business*

b. **Intonation** contours (marked by the presence of a stressed word) and **planning pauses** also provided useful guides. These, of course, require a commentator to listen to the recorded version of the material rather than simply reviewing the script.

The exercise went on to identify a number of other linguistic features which needed to be taken into account if confusion was to be avoided. They included the status of various verb forms[2]:

- Participles may indicate a new IU:

    He got into the car, // carrying the case.

    Badly wounded, // he managed to get back to camp.

    But not when used as Noun Phrase modifiers (*The badly wounded man got back to camp*).

- Gerunds may also mark a new IU:

    millions of pounds have been spent recently // on creating what are called shared streets*

    they want to be able to walk safely on pavements // without worrying about traffic*.

a. Modals were treated as part of a single IU, despite the way in which they modify a basic idea:

    We had to pay a lot for the tickets.

A grey area was found in nouns which carry a verbal implicature:

    Without the possibility of getting home by bus // she had to take a taxi.

    In the full knowledge that the house was empty, // they broke in.

    He bought a gun, // for fear that he'd be burgled.

In addition, there were issues at clause level. It proved relatively easy to eliminate topic markers in presentational material:

    [It's partly to do with] the amount of meat we produce, but [it's also to do with] the way in which we produce it. As the world's population gets larger and larger, [it could be argued that] far too much of our land is given over to producing animal feed*.

---

[2] Some of the examples that follow (marked *) are taken from the scripts that were analysed; others were designed for this report with a view to making clear the problem illustrated

On the same principle, indirect speech seemed easy to class as a single IU. However, there were borderline cases where the first part of an utterance brought in a new element of self-expression or opinion:

> *Some commentators have calculated //[that] it takes seven kilograms of grain to produce one kilogram of meat*.*

Leaving aside the details, the conclusion from this stage of the study was that it is not possible to rely on a computer program to calculate information density simply by identifying main verbs. (Self-evidently, this would in any case mean checking the results to eliminate auxiliary verbs and modals as indicators of IUs, and distinguishing present participles from one-word gerunds). The evidence of the exercise was that quite sensitive decisions may have to be made at clause level that only an informed human language user can apply. In addition, the recording of the script cannot be entirely ignored, given the way in which intonation contours and planning pauses may help to mark out Idea Units.

Rater agreement

A set of criteria were devised, based upon the exploratory exercise just described, with examples added. The next stage of the study explored whether, using these guidelines, the two collaborators might be able to produce comparable IU counts across texts.

They independently classified IUs in three sample texts (see Appendix 2) that had formed part of the original exercise. There was a good degree of agreement between them on where the IU boundaries should fall (partly using intuition but mainly using the pre-established criteria). However, one commentator consistently reported more IUs than did the other (the overall difference was 12%) and correspondingly shorter IUs as measured in words. This led to some expansion of the original guidelines, mainly to take account of certain features found in the type of interactive dialogue that often features in L2 listening materials. The investigators agreed to:

- treat open-ended questions followed by answers as, in effect two IUs;
- treat 'yes/no' questions followed by answers as consisting of 2 IUs only if the respondent added new information;
- treat conditional sentences as, in principle, consisting of two IUs.

In addition, in the case of presentational monologues, the investigators noted the importance of recognising moments at which the speaker repeated, rephrased or summarised points made earlier. It is difficult to legislate for these incidents since rephrasing still presents the listener with cognitive demands in the form of deciding whether a statement revisits an earlier IU or introduces a new one.

JT prepared to apply these expanded guidelines to analyse a different and larger section of the Aptis scripts. Before he did so, the investigators revisited their classification of IUs in relation to the three original scripts, and this time reported a divergence of around only 5%. This suggested that, given clear guidelines and a degree of practice, item writers can indeed calculate the information density of a script with a high degree of consistency.

Information density and listening difficulty

JT went on to undertake an analysis of a total of fifteen pieces of recorded material from the samples: five scoring at B1 level, five at B2 level and five at C1. This exercise aimed to extend Field's (2013) findings. It did so in the number of sample scripts featured and in the use of more specific criteria for defining IUs. It also did so by studying materials designed for a test (Aptis) that aims to cover a range of levels within a single paper. A variety of speech event types was featured (monologue vs dialogue vs monologue with additional voices). The balance between these types was representative of the level-by-level mixture in the group of scripts as a whole.

The texts selected varied considerably in length, so the table below displays mean figures per text at each proficiency level. Information is also given on the types of speech event featured; and figures are included for the mean number of items for which test takers had to find answers. The number is inflated at B2 level by the inclusion of a task where seven items had to be classed as 'Speaker A/Speaker B/Not mentioned'.

Level	Type	Items	Mean words	Mean no. of IUs	Mean min IU (words)	Mean max IU (words)
B1	3D 2M	5	71.6	9.8	3.4	9.2
B2	3D3 2M 1MV	11	143	14.8	4.4	15.2
C1	M5	12	223.6	16	4.8	17.4

Column 2: D= dialogue M = monologue MV= monologue with additional voices

Table 4: Mean length and number of IUs in 15 scripts targeting 3 proficiency levels

The table illustrates ways in which the writer made use of text length to increase test difficulty. As text length increases, so does the number of IUs that a test taker has to handle in building a discourse representation. The table also shows how the range of IU word lengths grows from 3.4 – 9.2 at B1 level to 4.4 – 15.2 at B2 and then 4.8 – 17.4 at C1. Storing words in the mind for parsing thus becomes increasingly demanding.

Following the Field (2013) precedent, figures were calculated for the average number of words that had to be processed in order to create an IU, and for the average time of the IU-relevant sections in seconds. A new feature was that figures were also calculated i.e. for the average number of IUs that listeners had to process per question answered.

Level	Total words	IU s	Words per IU	Total time	Secs. per IU	Items	IUs per item
B1	358	49	**7.31**	195	**3.98**	5	**9.8**
B2	715	74	**9.66**	287	**3.88**	11	**6.73**
C1	1118	80	**13.97**	501	**6.26**	12	**6.67**

Table 5: Measures of information density in 15 scripts targeting 3 proficiency levels

The results obtained are shown in Table 5 and are strikingly similar to those reported by Field (2013). It is clear that, again, the main device for increasing processing demands lies not in how densely the IUs are packed but *in the length of the group of words that has to be parsed in order to arrive at an IU*. A similar effect is seen in the difference between the average times taken by an IU at B2 and C1 levels

The accounts given so far here and elsewhere suggest that longer utterances representing IUs are more demanding because a larger string of words needs to be held in the mind for the purposes of parsing. To this, one can add another comment based upon a closer examination of the materials. The shortest IU in the samples was 2 words long; the longest 17. An IU can be as short as *I agree* or as long as *It would seem that the two areas identified in the 19th century are simply a kind of crossroads for language*. Inevitably, a longer utterance often provides an IU that is more detailed and thus considerably harder to process and commit to memory.

The results displayed also bring a new angle to the analysis. It would seem that another technique used by item writers to heighten the demands of a particular piece of material is to increase *the frequency with which IUs are matched against items*. The test taker has to sustain a higher level of attention because of the greater likelihood that a particular IU will provide the information needed for an answer.

Conclusions and some reflections

The study reported here demonstrates that the notion of measuring the information density of a listening text is not as straightforward as it might seem. The linguistic and phonetic criteria proposed by Chafe (1980) provide concrete guidelines but do not serve in a failsafe way to identify each and every idea unit in a text.

Chafe's conclusions were based upon oral narratives. It is clear that everyday conversational speech raises additional issues of speaker intention and of speaker-listener interaction (particularly in the use of question and answer) that cannot simply be resolved by counting verbs and observing where planning pauses fall. Similarly, in conversational speech and to an even greater degree in presentational speech, there are likely to be occurrences of repetition, rephrasing and summarising of a given point, about which fine decisions have to be made. An even more complex issue that has not been addressed here is whether one ever can or should (for the sake of completeness) deal with information that is not specifically expressed but is clearly implied by a speaker. This kind of feature entails a sharp increase in the processing demands made of a listener.

At all events, one conclusion is unavoidable: that (whatever pundits might claim), a computational solution to measuring the information load of a script is simply not a possibility. At best, a program might count the number of finite verb forms; but even this kind of analysis would need close checking. More positively, the exercise did show that, through a combination of intuition and criteria based on experience, a high degree of consistency could potentially be achieved between item writers.

Perhaps the most important outcome of the study has been to confirm Field's (2013) finding that the simple term *information density* is misleading. The assumption that often appears to underlie it is that, in easier texts, information is more loosely presented, with lengthier expositions of individual IUs and a degree of redundancy which spaces out the information that needs to be processed. Conversely, one might expect IUs to be more concisely expressed in higher-level texts, with fewer words taken to express more complex ideas. Both notions have now been discredited. It is true that the quantity of information that test takers have to handle increases markedly as they move up through proficiency levels. But that is a by-product of the increased length of the recorded material. The density of IUs within each minute of recorded time does not increase.

One can, of course, still envisage instances where information density in the form of a high concentration of information is indeed an issue. One example is the way in which less experienced item writers designing scripts for multiple-choice tasks sometimes feel compelled to cram up to three distractors plus a key into a short clip of 15–30 seconds. Informationally dense texts (*I nearly bought the blue shirt. I looked at the green one. I finally decided on the yellow one though the red one was cheaper.*) are intrinsically unfair to test takers precisely because of the amount of information they have to process in a short period of time. However, these concerns relate quite specifically to limits on how much information can comfortably be processed *at lower levels*.

What this exercise indicated once again is that standard practice amongst experienced item writers appears to be to increase information load by increasing the number of words that constitute an IU. This is entirely justifiable in cognitive terms; it fits in satisfyingly with evidence (reported earlier) that lower proficiency learners have to focus much of their limited resources of attention on processing at word and phrase level, and thus have problems in retaining anything more than small groups of words in their mind for parsing purposes. Hence the recommendation made in Chapter 4 that item writers should control for utterance length. Higher-level listeners, able to process L2 speech much more automatically, have no such problems and can retain much larger sets of words.

What the exercise has added to previous comment in the area is
- the argument that longer IUs are more likely to be more detailed and for that reason not only harder to parse but also harder to process and recall;
- the suggestion that a further expedient employed by item writers when attempting to increase informational demands is the number of items that a test taker is required to answer. Four questions about a short clip require a listener to focus more intently on IUs than does one.

In what has necessarily been a brief discussion of how information load is handled by item writers, the focus has been upon information density (however the term is interpreted) rather than information complexity.

But some mention of complexity should perhaps be made. The most obvious means of manipulating complexity lies in the logical links between one IU and the next, which enable test takers to trace the line of argument that holds a listening passage together and thus to build a discourse representation. One way of controlling the difficulty of these links is simply by relying on the discourse types that are conventionally favoured at different levels (see Chapter 4). At lower proficiency levels, the use of narrative and instructional texts provides simple chronological connections which are easy to follow. At higher levels, there may well be discursive texts where the connections (often expressed in the form of linkers) are based upon more complex relationships such as concession, addition, cause, result, etc.

Within the group of linkers, it might seem desirable to separate out those that represent relatively simple conceptual relationships from those that are more difficult to grasp and internalise. This, in fact, is rather more complicated than it might appear. To be sure, a corpus analyst is capable of creating a program that not only identifies linkers in a text and thus the amount of subordination, but also reports the frequency of individual linkers. However, measuring how often a linker occurs by no means tells us how relatively demanding it is for a test taker to follow the logical connection that the linker indicates.

Furthermore, the most demanding types of connection may well not involve linkers at all. There are many instances when a speaker chooses not to use a word or phrase to link two IUs explicitly; but relies upon the listener's ability to *infer the connection*. This would seem to add considerably to the processing demands imposed upon a test taker and to the challenge of constructing a discourse representation. However, it is again something that cannot be measured computationally. On the contrary: it entails highly subjective judgements where even the best-informed human discourse analysts are likely to disagree on the factors that make for difficulty.

One has to conclude that the issue of information complexity may be so intractable that it is not possible in this case to devise detailed guidelines to assist item writers. They have, quite simply, to rely upon their own experience and instinct concerning the relative demands imposed by various types of conceptual link.

12 Final remarks

A major goal of this book has been to challenge the testing community (test developers, item writers, stakeholders) to reflect on precisely what it is that we are testing when we test second language listening. With this in mind, the discussion opened with an outline of the processes that skilled first language listening entails. In the course of the book, that profile of listening (and the associated principle of approaching tests from the perspective of the test taker) has served a number of purposes.

- It has been used to draw the reader's attention to the demands that are present in all listening – and thus to shed light on the processes L2 listeners have to acquire.
- It has contributed to a set of descriptors (Chapter 3) that distinguish performance at different proficiency levels. The guiding principle was that it is only when learners develop automaticity in the basic perceptual processes that they have enough attention spare to engage in more sophisticated processes, such as interpreting what they have heard and building it into a wider line of argument.
- It has provided insights into some of the processes that any test of listening requires of its candidates: processes such as recognising words in connected speech or holding a group of those words in the mind in order to trace a grammatical pattern in them. By identifying more closely with the test taker, one is able to recognise the effect of features such as length of utterance or density of information upon performance (Chapter 4).
- It has raised questions (Chapter 7) about the way in which the task demands of conventional test formats require quite complex mental operations that take us beyond what listening normally requires.
- It has led to the idea (Chapter 8) that a model of this kind can assist testers to design items that target specific processes within listening. The challenge is to ensure that a test achieves as wide a spread as possible of those processes to ensure that it is fully representative of the skill that it aims to assess.
- A model like this also enables us to evaluate whether an existing test serves its purpose. Does the behaviour which it elicits from

its candidates resemble closely enough the processes which they would have to employ in a real-world context? In other words, can the test claim to be truly predictive of the candidate's performance in the world outside the test centre?

Alongside the account of the *processes* in which all listeners engage, there was also consideration of the *strategies* that language learners, especially early-stage ones, need to employ in order to compensate for gaps in understanding. Strategic competence is sometimes neglected because of conventions that favour tightly grading the language used in a test. It was argued that it is desirable to test strategy use by the occasional inclusion of pieces of language that are beyond the likely knowledge of the test taker. This recreates the realities of everyday L2 communication, where the ability to engage in compensatory strategies may be a crucial asset.

That said, a distinction needs to be made between communication strategies and others that are not valid because they relate purely and simply to the test situation. It was suggested (Chapter 7) that these *test-wise* strategies are an unfortunate by-product of a number of conventions (some necessary, some perhaps not) concerning the way in which listening test material is delivered.

A second theme of the book has been the nature of the signal to which the listener is exposed, whether in a first or a second language. Much of the focus has been upon the features of English speech, though the principles apply to most other languages. The challenges offered by spoken input can never be ignored when designing a listening test or conducting research into listening assessment. There is a tendency amongst applied linguists to trace close parallels between listening and reading. This can be seriously misleading so far as perceptual processes are concerned. At various points in the book, attention has been drawn to the ways in which decoding connected speech differs markedly from decoding written texts. With this in mind, Chapter 5 indicated how characteristics of the recorded material contribute to text difficulty, alongside the more conventional markers of difficulty described in Chapter 4.

To sum up, important considerations are that:

- *Speech is transitory.* A listener cannot go back and check as a reader can. This means that listening is more approximate than reading and that hypotheses about what has been heard may sometimes not be resolved until several words later. For the tester, it means that items cannot tap in to the level of detail that items in reading tests might aim for.

- *Speakers vary*. Voices vary in pitch, in accent, in the rate at which they speak. The impact of this upon the difficulty of recorded material was discussed in some detail in Chapter 5.
- *Styles of speech vary*, in terms of presentational style vs conversational, in terms of formality vs informality, in terms of precision of delivery.
- Above all, *spoken word recognition* is entirely unlike the recognition of written words. Words in connected speech do not possess the kind of standard form that spelling confers. Speakers constantly modify them in the interests of articulating them more easily. Furthermore, while the stressed word in an intonation group may be prominent because of its emphasis and duration, many of its companions will not. This especially applies to function words – the most frequent words in a language but (particularly in English) the most difficult to recognise because of their weak quality and brief duration.

So where might the testing of listening go now? Given the *leitmotif* of this book, it will not come as a surprise if I express a hope that testers will build on their current interest in the mind of the test taker. The problem is of course that it is quite difficult to gain access to what goes on in that mind in a way that is rigorous enough to sustain research and future test development. One such approach has become quite well established in the past ten years. As mentioned in Chapter 1, the notion of *cognitive validity* (Glaser, 1992) has a reputable history in ascertaining whether (say) a test of physics assesses a candidate's ability to think like a physicist rather than just mastering a set of facts. The concept was extended to tests of language skills in a recent series of publications in the Cambridge English SiLT series (for listening, see Field, 2013, 2018). Over time, an approach has been developed which entails evaluating in a systematic way whether the characteristics of a test elicit from the test taker the types of language behaviour that would apply in a real-world context. Three questions have been proposed:

- To what extent are the processes elicited by the test *representative* of those that would apply in the real world?
- Do they represent those processes *comprehensively* enough?
- How sensitively have these processes been *graded* in relation to the capabilities of candidates at different levels of proficiency?

Of course, this approach simply enables one to evaluate an existing test. The big question remains: What can we do to ensure that a new test measures up to these criteria before it actually goes live? As noted in Chapter 8, the problems of investigating on-line test taker performance are considerable. However, it would seem inevitable that at some point testers will modify their present heavy reliance upon post-hoc statistical evidence and will increasingly seek to use trials to investigate how test takers respond to test formats, test conventions and above all to items that seek to target particular processes. The study of item targeting by Holzknecht et al. (2017) appears to set an interesting precedent.

So far, this summary has tended to imply that listening to a foreign language involves using a single route to understanding. However, if we do indeed wish to identify with the position of the test taker, then it is essential to recognise that the needs of some groups of individuals differ markedly from those of the general population. As outlined in Chapter 9, they may have specific educational or professional reasons for taking a test. In this case, the test materials available should accurately reflect the types of listening process in which they will have to engage in *their* real world (e.g. receiving oral instruction in the case of the student or receiving, recording and responding to patient information in the case of the nurse). At present, far too many of these groups are assessed by means of general tests of listening which cannot predict reliably how they will perform when they arrive in post.

A parallel case is that of young L2 learners, also mentioned in Chapter 9. Listening tests designed for this population do indeed take account of their assumed interests: they feature bright pictures, simple rubrics, slow-paced recordings on familiar themes. But it is only relatively recently that thought has also been given to whether and how the child's stage of cognitive and L1 language development should be a factor in the types of task that are chosen and the types of language that are used.

Another likely development in tests of listening is the increased use of transmission by computer. The advantages of Computer Based Testing to test providers and test takers alike have been mentioned; and, as noted in Chapter 9, CBT also offers a potential solution to many of the problems associated with the pre-presentation of test questions. The use of CBT for listening assessment has only been briefly discussed in these pages for the reason that it appears to be going through a developmental phase. Some of the conventional formats used in the testing of listening do not adapt well to the small screen (for example, with a set of eight or ten MCQ items, a test taker faces a very small font and/or has to scroll down extensively). In principle, an interesting set of alternative formats could be used, including drag-and-drop and the ticking of boxes. But the platforms currently used by test providers are not always capable of identifying a correct answer in terms of its position on the screen. There is work in progress on this. There may also be developments in the scoring of multi-level tests, where the use of an *adaptive algorithm* would enable a computer to adjust the listening material delivered to reflect the test taker's scoring patterns so far.

It is not just the testing of second language listening but also much of the teaching that is likely to be computer-delivered in future. The great advantage of this medium is that a learner can take control of a recording and replay it as often as necessary, thus tackling his/her own personal problems of decoding and comprehension. Some materials allow learners to test themselves: attempting to transcribe what they hear, listening several times and then comparing the correct version. In this way, they can potentially diagnose their own listening problems. Harding, Alderson and Brunfaut (2015) extend this notion and make a case for specially designed diagnostic tests that would assist the process of detecting and resolving difficulties. This supports an earlier proposal by Field (2008a: 86–95) who argues strongly for instructors to enquire into the source of learners' mistakes in order to identify precisely why understanding has broken down. Small-scale remedial exercises then become possible – targeting the very processes that were described at the beginning of this book.

APPENDIX A

Examples of processes contributing to listening
(Field, 2008a: 336–339)

Decoding processes

1. *Phoneme level*
   Phoneme recognition in a range of contexts(?)

2. *Syllable level*
   Recognising syllable structure
   Recognising syllable stress and treating stressed syllables as more reliable
   Using stressed syllables as codes to identify words
   Using weak syllables to locate function words

3. *Word level*
   Lexical access: word form to word meaning
   Lexical segmentation
   Recognising variant forms of words
   Recognising complete formulaic chunks
   Using awareness of word frequency
   Words recently heard and active in the mind
   Words within the same set as those heard recently
   Distinguishing known and unknown words
   Dealing with unknown words: infer – generalise – ignore

4. *Syntactic parsing*
   Building syntactic structures as syllables are heard
   Using probability
   Using common chunks of language
   Using the verb to guess the pattern that will follow
   Checking guesses about what the final structure will be
   Distinguishing planning and hesitation pauses
   Using planning pauses and intonation groups to identify where a structure ends

5. *Intonation level*
>   Relating intonation groups to syntactic structure
>   Using the intonation group to check that words have been heard correctly
>   Treating focally stressed syllables as central to the message (and more reliable)
>   Recognising recurrent chunks
>   Guessing words of low prominence in the intonation group
>   Guessing speaker intentions that are expressed by intonation

6. *Normalisation to speaker voices*
>   Allowing for voice variation caused by gender and size of vocal tract
>   Setting baseline for loudness and pitch level,
>   Identifying speech rate
>   Drawing on a repertoire of known accents

Meaning based processes

1. *Word meaning*

   Identifying one of two or more possible senses of a word that fits the surrounding words or context

   Dealing with word ambiguity (e.g. homophones)

   Inferring the meaning of unknown words

2. *Syntactic meaning*

   Relating syntax to the context

   Interpreting a speaker's functional intentions

   Using function words and syntactic patterns to clarify what is heard

3. *Intonation meaning*

   Recognising given / new relationships

   Distinguishing contrastive and emphatic stress

   Relating contrastive and emphatic focal stress to preceding comments

   Recognising the end of an intonation group

   Recognising the end of a speaker's turn

   Using intonation to identify questions in statement form

   Distinguishing neutral – emotive – tentative intonations

4. *Using contextual knowledge*

   world knowledge – topic knowledge – knowledge of the speaker – knowledge of situation – knowledge of setting – knowledge of current and ongoing topics

5. *Using schemas and scripts*

   Predicting what will be said

   Using topic to activate vocabulary

   Inferring what the speaker has not expressed

   Allowing for culturally determined schemas

6. *Context / co-text and meaning*

   Using context and co-text to narrow down word meaning

   Using context and co-text to infer unexpressed meaning

   Using context and co-text to infer word meaning

7. *Using inference*

   Inferring information the speaker has left unsaid

   Inferring connections between pieces of information that were not made explicitly

8. *Making reference connections*
    Carrying forward a current topic
    Dealing with imprecise reference

9. *Interpreting the utterance*
    Interpreting speaker language
    Interpreting speaker intentions

10. *Selecting information*
    Considering relevance
    Considering redundancy: addition versus repetition
    Dealing with incoherence

11. *Integrating information*
    Connecting new information to previous
    Recognising locally connecting linkers
    Recognising 'signpost' linkers
    Inferring links not marked by linkers
    Monitoring to ensure that what has been understood so far is
    correct
    Recognising a structure in the discourse
    Distinguishing topics from sub-topics
    Recognising conventional patterns of discourse

12. *Forming and checking provisional discourse representations*
    Forming the base for a discourse representation
    Adding new information as it arrives
    Checking, revising and upgrading the discourse representation

APPENDIX B

Sample Scripts

Level   B1+

Script   *P: Listen to this radio broadcast about office workers' lunches. What is the main point?*

M: the **long** lunch hour has been replaced by the **sandwich** ++ according to a new **survey** ++ most people take just **30** minutes + to **eat** in the middle of the day + many of us don't even **leave** our **desks**

F: er I'm taking an **hour** today + but it's normally sort of **half** an hour or **20 minutes.**

M1: I pop out for about **ten minutes** + get something to **eat** + and then go back to my **desk**

M: a **survey** at the start of the **year** + found that only **one** per cent of people in Britain + **regularly** take a full 60 minute break + this is very **different** from forty years ago + when offices everywhere **stopped work** at one o'clock + people went **out** to lunch + and didn't return until two.

Task   [APPEARS ON SCREEN BETWEEN TWO PLAYS]

Now listen again to the broadcast. What is the MAIN point? Choose A, B, C or D.

Compared with 40 years ago

    A. office workers eat snacks these days
    B. people eat lunch earlier
    C. lunch breaks are much shorter
    D. office workers stay at their desks at lunchtime

Process   **Identify main point. Material authentic in origin**

Level   C1

Script   *P: Listen to a talk by a blind woman about the problems that blind people have in cities. What are the two types of problem?*

F: I want to talk to you about the **state** of our **pavements** + because walking the streets if you're **blind** or partially sighted + can be a pretty **dangerous** business + it's reckoned that **many** people with poor eyesight + **never leave home alone** + and that the **state** of our **streets** is a big part of the reason why ++ as long ago as **1978** + blind people started a **campaign** called Give Us Back our **Pavements** + but many of the hazards are **still** there or have got **worse** ++ it's not just about **damaged pavements** with broken **paving** stones + **millions** of pounds have been spent recently on creating + what are called **shared** streets + where there are no **longer** pavements that separate **pedestrians** from **cars** + town planners have even got rid of **safe crossings** for pedestrians ++ if you watch **videos** about these shared streets in **Denmark** or the **Netherlands** + you won't see any **blind** people + why? + because **architects** and planners haven't **consulted** them + **blind** and **partially** sighted people + want to be able to walk **safely** on pavements + without worrying about **traffic**

Task   [APPEARS ON SCREEN BETWEEN TWO PLAYS]

Now listen again to the speaker and identify the two problems faced by blind people in cities. Choose A, B, C or D.

The first problem is that people with poor sight

A. don't like going out.
B. can fall over on damaged pavements.
C. can walk into streets where there are dangerous criminals.
D. need more pavements to walk on.

The second problem is that in shared streets

A. blind people cannot avoid crowds.
B. architects do not allow enough space.
C. blind people cannot see where safe crossings are.
D. traffic is not separated from pedestrians.

Process   **Use inference to identify two main points.**
Material authentic in origin

Level   C1

Script   *P: You will hear a talk about eating meat. What is the argument against it?*

M: there are people who say that meat's an important part of our diet ++ according to them, human beings are meat-eaters + which is why vegetarians have to take extra vitamin pills to keep healthy ++ well, that's all very well + but consider the facts + in order to produce the meat + we have to feed the animals + it's been calculated that we need seven kilograms of grain + to produce one kilogram of meat + a pretty shocking statistic given that many people in the world don't have enough to eat + so why not eat less meat and give the grain to human beings instead? ++ the farmers answer that much of what cows and sheep eat comes from open grassland + they also say that fields producing food for cows and sheep couldn't be used to produce the grain that human beings use in bread or flour.

Task   [APPEARS ON SCREEN BETWEEN TWO PLAYS]

Now you will hear the talk again. What argument for eating less meat does the speaker mention?

    A. To produce meat we have to kill animals.
    B. Many people in the world cannot afford meat
    C. It takes too much grain to feed the animals
    D. Open grassland is destroyed by farm animals

Process   **Identify speaker's viewpoint in a discursive text**
Material: scripted

REFERENCES

Bachman, L.F. (1990). *Fundamental considerations in language testing.* Oxford: Oxford University Press.

Bates, E. & MacWhinney, B. (1989). Functionalism and the competition model. In B. MacWhinney & E. Bates (Eds.), *The cross-linguistic study of sentence processing* (pp. 3–76). New York: Cambridge University Press.

Bekleyen, N. (2009). Helping teachers become better English students: Causes, effects, and coping strategies for foreign language listening anxiety, *System* 37(4), 664–675.
https://doi.org/10.1016/j.system.2009.09.010

Berry, V., O'Sullivan, B. & Rugea, S. (2013). *Identifying the appropriate IELTS score levels for IMG applicants to the GMC register.* London: General Medical Council. Retrieved from:
https://www.gmc-uk.org/-/media/about/identifying-the-appropriate-ielts-score-levels-for-img-applicants-to-the-gmc-register.pdf

Blakemore, S-J. (2007). The social brain of a teenager. Spearman Medal lecture to the British Psychological Society, *The Psychologist* 20, 600–602.

Blau, E. (1990). The effect of syntax, speed and pauses on listening comprehension. *TESOL Quarterly*, 24(4), 746–753.
https://doi.org/10.2307/3587129

Bloomfield, A., Wayland, S.C., Rhodes, E., Blodgett, A., Linck, J. & Ross, S. (2010). *What makes listening difficult?* College Park, Maryland: University of Maryland.

Brindley, G. & Slatyer, H. (2002). Exploring task difficulty in ESL listening assessment. *Language Testing*, 19(4), 369–394.
https://doi.org/10.1191/0265532202lt236oa

Brown, G. & Yule, G. (1983). *Discourse analysis.* Cambridge: Cambridge University Press. https://doi.org/10.1017/CBO9780511805226

Brown, G. (1990). *Listening to spoken English* (2nd ed.). Harlow: Longman.

Buck, G. (1990). *The testing of second language listening comprehension.* Unpublished Ph.D. dissertation. Lancaster University, Lancaster.

Buck, G. (2001). *Assessing listening.* Cambridge: Cambridge University Press. https://doi.org/10.1017/CBO9780511732959

Butterworth, B. (1980). Evidence from pauses in speech, In B. Butterworth (Ed.), *Language production: Vol. 1. Speech and talk* (pp. 155–176). London: Academic Press.

Bybee, J. (2001). *Phonology and language use.* Cambridge: Cambridge University Press. https://doi.org/10.1017/CBO9780511612886

Calvert, D.R. (1986). *Descriptive phonetics* (2nd ed.). New York: Thieme.

Canagarajah, S. (2006). Changing communicative needs, revised assessment objectives: testing English as an international language, *Language Assessment Quarterly*, 3(3), 229–242. https://doi.org/10.1207/s15434311laq0303_1

Canale, M. & Swain, M. (1980). Theoretical bases of communicative approaches to second language teaching and testing, *Applied Linguistics* 1(1), 1–47.

Chafe, W.L. (1979). The flow of thought and the flow of language. In T. Givon (Ed.), *Syntax and semantics, 12: Discourse and syntax* (pp. 159–181). New York: Academic Press.

Chafe, W.L. (1980). *The Pear stories: Cognitive, cultural, and linguistic aspects of narrative production.* Norwood, NJ: Ablex.

Clopper, C.G. & Pisoni, D.B. (2008). Perception of dialect variation. In D.B. Pisoni & R.E. Remez (Eds.), *The handbook of speech perception* (pp. 313–337). Oxford: Blackwell.

Cohen, A. (1998). *Strategies of language learning and language use.* Harlow: Longman.

Coniam, D. (2001). The use of audio or video comprehension as an assessment instrument in the certification of English language teachers: A case study. *System*, 29(1), 1–14. https://doi.org/10.1016/S0346-251X(00)00057-9

Council of Europe (2001). *Common European framework of reference for languages: Learning, teaching, assessment.* Cambridge: Cambridge University Press.

Croft, W. (1995). Intonation units and grammatical structure. *Linguistics*, 33(5), 839–882. https://doi.org/10.1515/ling.1995.33.5.839

Cutler, A. and Clifton, C. (1999). Comprehending spoken language: A blueprint of the listener. In C.M. Brown & P. Hagoort (Eds.), *The neurocognition of language* (pp. 123–166). Oxford: Oxford University Press.

Donaldson, M. (2006). *Children's minds.* London: Harper Perennial.

Ducasse, A.M. & Brown, A. (2009). Assessing paired orals: Raters' orientation to interaction. *Language Testing* 26(3), 423–443. https://doi.org/10.1177/0265532209104669

Elliott, M. & Wilson, J. (2013). Context validity. In A. Geranpayeh & L. Taylor (Eds.), *Examining listening* (pp. 152–241). Cambridge: Cambridge University Press.

Erlam, R.M. (2006). Elicited imitation as a measure of L2 implicit knowledge: An empirical validation study. *Applied Linguistics*, 27(3), 464–491. https://doi.org/10.1093/applin/aml001

Field, J. (2004). An insight into listeners' problems: Too much bottom-up or too much top-down?' *System*, 32(3), 363–77. https://doi.org/10.1016/j.system.2004.05.002

Field, J. (2008a). *Listening in the language classroom*. Cambridge: Cambridge University Press.

Field, J. (2008b). Bricks or mortar: Which parts of the input does a second language listener rely on? *TESOL Quarterly*, 42(3), 411–432. https://doi.org/10.1002/j.1545-7249.2008.tb00139.x

Field, J. (2008c). The L2 listener: Type or individual? In H. Hendriks (Ed.), *Working papers in English and applied linguistics* (pp. 11–32). RCEAL, Cambridge University.

Field, J. (2011). Into the mind of the academic listener. *Journal of EAP* 10(2), 102–112. https://doi.org/10.1016/j.jeap.2011.04.002

Field, J. (2012a). The cognitive validity of the lecture-based question in the IELTS listening paper. In L. Taylor & C.J. Weir (Eds.), *IELTS collected papers 2: Research in reading and listening assessment,* (Studies in language testing, Vol. 34, pp. 391–453). Cambridge: Cambridge University Press.

Field, J. (2012b). *The cognitive validity of the CAE listening test as a predictor of academic performance.* Unpublished Report on project funded by Cambridge ESOL Research and Validation Unit 2011.

Field, J. (2013). Cognitive validity. In A. Geranpayeh & L. Taylor (Eds.), *Examining listening* (pp. 77–151). Cambridge: Cambridge University Press.

Field, J. (2014a). Myth: Pronunciation teaching needs to fix in the minds of learners a set of distinct consonant and vowel sounds. In L. Grant, (Ed.), *Pronunciation myths* (pp. 80–106). Ann Arbor: University of Michigan Press.

Field, J. (2014b). *Standards for second language listening in the Rwandan primary classroom.* Unpublished report. Kigali, Rwanda: British Council and Rwanda Education Board.

Field, J. (2015). *The effects of single and double play upon listening test outcomes and cognitive processing* (ARAGS research reports online, AR-G/2015/003). Retrieved from https://www.britishcouncil.org/sites/default/files/field.pdf

Field, J. (2018). The cognitive validity of tests of listening and speaking designed for young learners. In S. Papp & S. Rixon (Eds.), *Examining young learners: Research and practice in assessing the English of school-age learners* (pp. 128–200). Cambridge: Cambridge University Press.

Freedle, R. & Kostin, I. (1999). Does the text matter in a multiple-choice test of comprehension? The case for the construct validity of TOEFL's minitalks. *Language Testing,* 16(1), 2–32.

Galaczi, E.D. (2014). Interactional competence across proficiency levels: How do learners manage interaction in paired speaking tests? *Applied Linguistics,* 35(5): 553–574. https://doi.org/10.1093/applin/amt017

Gathercole, S.E. & Baddeley, A. (1993). *Working memory and language.* Hove: Erlbaum.

Geranpayeh, A. & Taylor, L. (2008). Examining listening: Developments and issues in assessing second language listening. *Cambridge ESOL Research Notes,* 32: 2–5.

Gimson, A.C. (1989). *An introduction to the pronunciation of English* (4th ed.). London: Hodder Arnold.

Gimson, A.C. (2008). *Gimson's pronunciation of English* (7th ed., revised A. Cruttenden). London: Hodder Education.

Ginther, A. (2002). Context and content visuals and performance on listening comprehension stimuli. *Language Testing,* 19(2), 133–167. https://doi.org/10.1191/0265532202lt225oa

Glaser, R. (1991). Expertise and assessment. In M.C. Wittrock & E.L. Baker (Eds.), *Testing and cognition* (pp. 17–30). Englewood Cliffs, Prentice Hall.

Goldinger, S.D. (1997). Speech perception and production in an episodic lexicon. In K. Johnson & J.W. Mullennix (Eds.), *Talker variability in speech processing* (pp. 33–66). New York: Academic Press.

Goldman-Eisler, F. (1968). *Psycholinguistics: Experiments in spontaneous speech.* London: Academic Press.

Goswami, U. (1998). *Cognition in children.* Hove: Psychology Press.

Goswami, U. (2006). *Cognitive development: Critical concepts in psychology.* London: Routledge.

Green, K.P. (1998). The use of auditory and visual information during phonetic processing: Implications for theories of speech perception. In R. Campbell & B. Dodd (Eds.), *Hearing by eye II: Advances in the psychology of speechreading and audiovisual speech* (pp. 3–25). Hove: Psychology Press.

Griffiths, R. (1992). Speech rate and listening comprehension: Further evidence of the relationship. *TESOL Quarterly,* 26(2), 385–391. https://doi.org/10.2307/3587015

Grosjean, F. & Gee, J. (1987). Prosody structure and spoken word recognition. *Cognition*, 25(1–2):135–155.
https://doi.org/10.1016/0010-0277(87)90007-2

Grosjean, F. (1985). The recognition of words after their acoustic offsets: Evidence and implications. *Perception and Psychophysics*, 38(4), 299–310. https://doi.org/10.3758/BF03207159

Harding, L. (2011). *Accent and listening assessment*. Frankfurt: Peter Lang.

Harding, L., Alderson. J.C. & Brunfaut, T. (2015). Diagnostic assessment of reading and listening in a second or foreign language: Elaborating on diagnostic principles. *Language Testing* 3(3), 317–336.
https://doi.org/10.1177/0265532214564505

Hawkins, S. (1999). Re-evaluating assumptions about speech perception: Interactive and integrative theories. In J.M. Pickett (Ed.), *The acoustics of speech communication: Fundamentals, speech perception theory, and technology* (pp. 232–288). Needham Heights, MA: Allyn and Bacon.

Holzknecht, F., Eberharter, K., Kremmel, B., McCray, G., Zehentner, M., Konrad, E. & Spöttl, C. (2017). *Looking into listening: Using eye-tracking to establish the cognitive validity of the Aptis Listening test.* (ARAGs research reports online, AR-G/2018/4). Retrieved from https://www.britishcouncil.org/sites/default/files/looking_into_listening.pdf.

In'nami, Y. & Koizumi, R. (2009). A meta-analysis of test format effects on reading and listening test performance: Focus on multiple-choice and open-ended formats. *Language Testing*, 26(2), 219–244.
https://doi.org/10.1177/0265532208101006

Ingram, D. & Bayliss, A. (2007). IELTS as a predictor of academic language performance, Part 1. *IELTS research reports*, 7(3), 1–68.

Jenkins, J. (2000). *The phonology of English as an international language*. Oxford: Oxford University Press.

Jensen, C. & Hansen, C. (1995). The effect of prior knowledge on EAP listening-test performance. *Language Testing*, 12(1), 99–119.
https://doi.org/10.1177/026553229501200106

Johnson, K. (2008). Speaker normalisation in speech perception. In D.B. Pisoni & R.E. Remez, (Eds.), *The handbook of speech perception* (pp. 363–389). Oxford: Blackwell.

Jusczyk. P.W. (2000). *The discovery of spoken language*. Boston, MA: MIT Press.

Laufer, B. (1989). What percentage of text is essential for comprehension?. In C. Lauren & M. Nordman (Eds.), *Special language from humans thinking to thinking machines* (pp. 316–323). Clevedon: Multilingual Matters.

Laver, J. (1994). *Principles of phonetics*. Cambridge: Cambridge University Press. https://doi.org/10.1017/CBO9781139166621

Levelt, W.J.M. (1989). *Speaking: From interaction to articulation*. Cambridge, MA: MIT Press.

Lynch, T. (2009). *Teaching second language listening*. Oxford: Oxford University Press.

Macaro, E., Graham, S. & Vanderplank, R. (2007). A review of listening strategies: Focus on sources of knowledge and on success. In A.D. Cohen & E. Macaro (Eds.), *Language learner strategies* (pp. 165–185). Oxford: Oxford University Press.

Major, R.C., Fitzmaurice, S.F., Ferenc, B. & Balasubramanian, C. (2002). The effects of nonnative accents on listening comprehension: Implications for ESL assessment. *TESOL Quarterly*, 36(2), 173–190. https://doi.org/10.2307/3588329

Martin, W. (1988). Variation in lexical frequency. In P. van Reenen & K. van Reenen-Stein (Eds.), *Distributions spatiales et temporelles, constellations des manuscrits/Spatial and temporal distributions, manuscript constellations* (pp. 139–152). Amsterdam: John Benjamins. https://doi.org/10.1075/z.37.16mar

Martinez, R. & Schmitt, N. (2012). A phrasal expressions list. *Applied Linguistics* 33(3), 299–320. https://doi.org/10.1093/applin/ams010

Massaro, D.W. (1974). Perceptual units in speech recognition. *Journal of Experimental Psychology*, 102(2), 349–353. https://doi.org/10.1037/h0035854

Mattys S.L. & Melhorn J.F. (2005). How do syllables contribute to the perception of spoken English? Insight from the migration paradigm. *Language and Speech*, 48(2), 223–52. https://doi.org/10.1177/00238309050480020501

May, L. (2007). *Interaction in a paired speaking test: The rater's perspective*. Unpublished PhD dissertation, University of Melbourne, Melbourne, Australia.

McCarthy, M. & Carter, R. (1997). Written and spoken vocabulary. In N. Schmitt & M. McCarthy (Eds.), *Vocabulary: Description, acquisition and pedagogy* (pp. 20–39). Cambridge: Cambridge University Press.

Meadows, S. (2006). *The child as thinker*. Hove: Psychology Press. https://doi.org/10.4324/9780203134009

Milton, J. & Hopkins, N. (2006). Comparing phonological and ortho-graphic vocabulary size: Do vocabulary tests underestimate the vocab-ulary knowledge of some learners? *Canadian Modern Language Review*, 63(1), 127–147. https://doi.org/10.21832/9781847692092

Milton, J. (2009). *Measuring second language vocabulary acquisition.* Bristol, UK: Multilingual Matters.

Milton, J., Wade, J. & Hopkins, N. (2010). Aural word recognition and oral comprehension in a foreign language. In R. Chacón-Beltrán, C. Abello-Contess & M. Torreblanca-López (Eds.), *Insights into non-native vocabulary teaching and learning* (pp. 83–98). Clifton: Multilingual Matters. https://doi.org/10.21832/9781847692900-007

Nakatsuhara, F. (2011). Effects of the number of participants on group oral test performance. *Language Testing*, 28(4): 483–508. https://doi.org/10.1177/0265532211398110

Nakatsuhara, F. (2012). The relationship between test-takers' listening proficiency and their performance on the IELTS Speaking test. In L. Taylor and C.J. Weir (Eds.), *IELTS collected papers 2: Research in reading and listening assessment* (pp. 519–573). Cambridge: Cambridge University Press.

Nakatsuhara, F. and Field, J. (2012). *A study of examiner interventions in relation to the listening demands they make on candidates in the GESE exams*, Project report, Trinity College London.

Nation, I.S.P. (2001). *Learning vocabulary in another language.* Cambridge: Cambridge University Press. https://doi.org/10.1017/ CBO9781139524759

Nygaard, L.C. (2008). Linguistic and nonlingusitic properties of speech. In D.B. Pisoni & R.E. Remez (Eds.), *The handbook of speech per-ception* (pp. 390–413). Oxford: Blackwell. https://doi.org/10.3758/BF03206860

Nygaard, L.C. and Pisoni, D.B. (1998). Talker-specific perceptual learning in speech perception. *Perception and Psychophysics*, 60(3), 355–76.

O'Sullivan, B. (2011). Theories and practices in language testing. In P. Powell-Davies (Ed.), *New directions: Assessment and evaluation* (pp. 15–23). London: British Council.

Ockey, G.J. (2007). Construct implications of including still image or video in computer-based listening tests. *Language Testing*, 24(4), 517–537. https://doi.org/10.1177/0265532207080771

Pashler, H. and Johnston, J.C. (1998). Attentional limitations in dual task performance. In H. Pashler (Ed.), *Attention* (pp. 155–189). Hove: Psychology Press.

Peterson, G.E. & Barney, H.L. (1952). Control methods used in a study of the vowels. *Journal of the Acoustical Society of America*, 24, 175–84. https://doi.org/10.1121/1.1906875

Pisoni, D.B. (1997). Some thoughts on "normalization" in speech perception, in K. Johnson, K. Mullennix & J.W. Mullennix (Eds.), *Talker variability in speech processing* (pp. 33–66). San Diego: Academic Press.

Ramsaran, S. (1978). *Phonetic and phonological correlates of style in English: A preliminary investigation.* Unpublished PhD dissertation. University of London, London.

Richards, J. (1983). Listening comprehension: approach, design, procedure. *TESOL Quarterly*, 17(2), 219–39. https://doi.org/10.2307/3586651

Roach, P. (2000). *English phonetics and phonology* (3rd ed.). Cambridge: Cambridge University Press.

Rost, M. (1992). *Listening in language learning.* London: Longman.

Ruhm, R., Leitner-Jones, C., Kulmhofer, A, Kiefer, T., Mlakar, H. & Itzlinger-Bruneforth, U. (2016). Playing the recording once or twice: Effects on listening test performances, *International Journal of Listening*, 30(1–2), 67–83. https://doi.org/10.1080/10904018.2015.1104252

Salisbury, K. (2005). *The edge of expertise: Towards an understanding of listening test item writing as professional practice.* Unpublished PhD dissertation, Kings College London.

Schmidt-Rinehart, B.C. (1994). The effects of topic familiarity on second language listening comprehension. *Modern Language Journal*, 78(2): 179–189. https://doi.org/10.1111/j.1540-4781.1994.tb02030.x

Schneider, W. & Lockl, K. (2002). The development of metacognitive knowledge in children and adolescents. In T.J. Perfect & B.L. Schwartz (Eds.), *Applied metacognition* (pp. 224–257). Cambridge: Cambridge University Press.

Sedgwick, C., Garner, M. & Vicente-Macia, I. (2016). Investigating the language needs of international nurses: Insiders' perspectives. *IELTS reports online series*, 2016 (2), 1–38.

Sherman, J. (1997). The effect of question preview in listening comprehension tests. *Language Testing*, 14(2), 185–213. https://doi.org/10.1177/026553229701400204

Staehr, L.S. (2008). Vocabulary size and the skills of listening, reading and writing. *Language Learning Journal*, 36(2), 139–152. https://doi.org/10.1080/09571730802389975

Styles, E. (2006). *The psychology of attention* (2nd ed.). New York: Taylor & Francis.

Sueyoshi, A. & Hardison, D.M. (2005). The role of gesture and facial cues in second language listening comprehension. *Language Learning*, 55(4): 661–699. https://doi.org/10.1111/j.0023-8333.2005.00320.x

Suvarov, R. (2009). Context visuals in L2 listening tests: the effects of photographs and video vs. audio-only format. In C.A. Chapelle, H.G. Jun & I. Katz (Eds.), *Developing and evaluating language learning materials* (pp. 53–68). Ames, IA: Iowa State University.

Suvarov, R. (2015). *Interacting with visuals in L2 listening tests: An eye-tracking study* (ARAGs research reports online, Vol. AR-A/2015/1). Retrieved from https://www.britishcouncil.org/exam/aptis/research/publications/interacting

Tanenhaus, M.K. & Trueswell, J.C. (1995). Sentence comprehension. In J.L. Miller & P.D. Eimas (Eds.), *Speech language and communication* (pp. 217–262). San Diego: Academic Press. https://doi.org/10.1016/B978-012497770-9.50009-1

Tauroza, S. and Allison, D. (2000). Speech rates in British English, *Applied Linguistics* 11(1), 90–105. https://doi.org/10.1093/applin/11.1.90

Taylor, L. (2006). The changing landscape of English: Implications for language assessment. *ELT Journal*, 60(1), 51–60. https://doi.org/10.1093/elt/cci081

Taylor, L. (2009). Language varieties and their implications for testing and assessment. In L. Taylor, & C.J. Weir (Eds.), *Language testing matters: Investigating the wider social and educational impact of assessment*. Proceedings of the ALTE Cambridge conference, April 2008. (Studies in language testing, Vol. 31, pp. 139–157). Cambridge: UCLES/Cambridge University Press.

Taylor, L. (2013). Introduction. In A. Geranpayeh & L. Taylor (Eds.), *Examining listening* (pp. 1–35). Cambridge: Cambridge University Press.

Vandergrift, L. (1997). The Cinderella of communication strategies: Receptive strategies in interactive listening. *Modern Language Journal*, 81(4), 494–505. https://doi.org/10.1111/j.1540-4781.1997.tb05517.x

Weir, C. (2005). *Language testing and validation: An evidence-based approach.* Basingstoke: Palgrave Macmillan.
https://doi.org/10.1057/9780230514577

Weir, C.J. and Vidaković, I. (2013). The measurement of listening ability 1913–2012. In C.J. Weir, I. Vidaković & E. Galaczi (Eds.), *Measured constructs: A history of Cambridge English examinations* 1913–2012 (pp. 347–419). Cambridge: Cambridge University Press.

Wells, J.C. (1982). *Accents of English 3: Beyond the British Isles.* Cambridge: Cambridge University Press.
https://doi.org/10.1017/CBO9780511611759

Wickens, C.D. (1984). Processing resources in attention. In R. Parsuraman and D.R. Davies (Eds.), *Varieties of attention* (pp. 63–102). Orlando, FL, Academic Press.

Wray, A. (2001). *Formulaic language and the lexicon.* Cambridge: Cambridge University Press.

Wu, Y. (1998). What do tests of listening comprehension test? – A retrospection study of EFL test takers performing a multiple-choice task. *Language Testing,* 15(1), 21–44.

Yuill, N. and Oakhill, J. (1991). *Children's problems in text comprehension: An experimental investigation.* Cambridge: Cambridge University Press.

INDEX

CPSIA information can be obtained
at www.ICGtesting.com
Printed in the USA
LVHW060601080519
617017LV00004B/35/P